Praise for *The Subtle Art of Caring: A Guide*

In this beautifully illustrated and poetic book, F
with unfailing insight to that difficult place whei
practice meets the urgent global issues of our time. In conversation
with Buddhist activists, she shows how we can respond with loving-
kindness in its different forms to our own pain and the pain of the world.
An important read for the Anthropocene age. – **Akasharaja**, chair of
the Shrewsbury Buddhist centre and co-founder of the Triratna Earth
Sangha

In *The Subtle Art of Caring,* River, a passionate contemplative artist and
activist, shares with us what she has learned in her journey of creativity,
social engagement, and meditation. Using as a template the five qualities
of pausing, befriending, enjoying, caring, and letting be, she shows the
way to a profoundly beneficial life for ourselves and others. – **Martine
Batchelor**, meditation teacher and author of *Meditation for Life* and *Let
Go: A Buddhist Guide to Breaking Free of Habits*

This book is a tonic for our times. Read and respair (rebuild hope and
recover from despair)! I was invited into a different way of being as I
imbibed this beautiful collage of reflections, conversations, and creative
explorations – a way of being that honours the continuity between my
own wellbeing and that of all living things. – **Prof. Rebecca Crane**,
PhD, Director, Centre for Mindfulness Research and Practice, Bangor
University, UK

If you wish to explore how to take Buddhism off the meditation
cushion and into the world, read this book. The transformative words
and immersive images create a space for deep contemplation. River
Wolton uses philosophy, interviews, anecdotes, and humour to help us
compassionately meet today's social, racial, and ecological challenges
with mindful action. – **Dene Donalds**, Dharma teacher in the lineage of
Thich Nhat Hanh and a founding member of the Colours of Compassion
Sangha

In *The Subtle Art of Caring* River has written a courageous book that draws upon the richness of the teaching of the Buddha. With so much distress in the world we easily sink into despair or feelings of helplessness. River reveals the powerful ways we can contribute to the end of distress through transforming our own hearts. – **Christina Feldman**, co-founder of Gaia House and Bodhi College and the author of many books, including *Boundless Heart*

This is a beautiful book. River Wolton shares examples from her life and the lives of her friends to steer us through the labyrinth of caring in a seemingly uncaring world. With delightful illustrations and helpful creative exercises, she takes us into the world of the Brahma Viharas – a traditional Buddhist teaching – making it relevant and accessible for the world today. – **Dharmacharini Anagarika Parami**, senior teacher in the Triratna Buddhist Community, and ex-bereavement counsellor

River skilfully weaves her personal experiences of activism and witnessing to bring into focus the healing insight of self and collective care practices. Drawn from Buddhist wisdom, she stories how mindful awareness can transmute the inner and outer crises of distress and disconnection. A toolkit of creative explorations, rituals, and reflections, this important offering is both an invitation and an orientation towards deep care and kindness. This opportunity to pause and practise is a thoughtful and wise lodestar, a toolkit to orient and remind us to root ourselves in loving-kindness, compassion, sympathetic joy, and equanimity. – **Jennifer Radloff** is a South African who works at the intersection of feminist activism and the Internet, building infrastructures of care for self and collective healing responses to the traumas of our times

Compassion through the lens of an activist and poet allows us to delve deeper into some of the cries of the world. River Wolton creates tapestries woven with Dharma, illustrations, and diverse voices. This insightful book offers respite, reframing, and relief from habitual mindsets, giving radical rest to our neural pathways. – **Vimalasara**, author of *Eight Step Recovery*

The Subtle Art of Caring

A Guide to Sustaining Compassion

River Wolton

Illustrations by Emma Burleigh

For my parents
Jenny and Aubrey
from whom I learned to be curious.

Windhorse Publications
38 Newmarket Road
Cambridge CB5 8DT
info@windhorsepublications.com
windhorsepublications.com

Cover design by Katarzyna Manecka
Text design by Francesca Romano Design
Typesetting and layout by Tarajyoti
Printed by Bell & Bain Ltd, Glasgow

British Library Cataloguing in Publication Data:
A catalogue record for this book is available from the British Library.
ISBN 978-1-915342-21-8

CONTENTS

About the author and illustrator   VIII
Publisher's acknowledgements   X
Audio recordings   XI
Foreword   XIII

Introduction   1
Chapter 1   Pausing   21
Chapter 2   Befriending   51
Chapter 3   Enjoying   83
Chapter 4   Caring   107
Chapter 5   Letting be   141

Resource 1   The *Metta Sutta*   173
Resource 2   Reflections for sustaining compassion in daily life   175
Resource 3   Sustaining compassion with others   178

Glossary   182
Abbreviations   184
Selected references and further reading   185
Acknowledgements   188
Notes   190
About the contributors   199
Index   201

ABOUT THE AUTHOR AND ILLUSTRATOR

About the author

River Wolton trained as a social worker, psychotherapist, and carpenter; since 1998 she has taught creative writing in therapeutic, community, and educational settings. She is a former Derbyshire Poet Laureate, and her poetry collections include *Leap*, *Indoor Skydiving*, and *Year* – poems written each day of 2020 on the theme of kindness and obstacles to it.

A deepening interest in the connections between psychology, embodiment, creativity, activism, and spiritual practice led her to an Insight Meditation retreat in 2000. Since then she has been a regular retreatant at Gaia House, Devon, and continues to be inspired by teachings in the Buddhist tradition, and by radical thinkers who seek to address the crises of our times.

River helped to establish Sheffield Insight Meditation, completed Dharma Teacher Training with Bodhi College, and teaches meditation retreats and groups throughout the UK. A longtime peace, feminist, and LGBTQI+ activist, River sang for many years with lesbian acapella group Deep C Divas, and co-founded Out Aloud, Sheffield's LGBT+ choir.

About the illustrator

Emma Burleigh is an artist, illustrator, comics creator, and teacher. She is the author of two art coursebooks, *Soul Color* and *Earth Color*, which are designed to nurture mindfulness, creativity, and nature connectedness.

After experiencing burnout as an activist and schoolteacher in her twenties, Emma ended up at Gaia House, where she fell in love with the potential of Dharma practice to transform her world at both the personal and the collective level.

Emma first met River Wolton through a friend at Gaia House, and soon after that they decided to work together, exploring ways of combining River's words with Emma's images. This book is their third collaboration.

You can find out more about Emma and her artwork at www.emmaburleigh.com.

PUBLISHER'S ACKNOWLEDGEMENTS

Windhorse Publications wish to gratefully acknowledge a grant from the Future Dharma Fund and the Triratna European Chairs' Assembly Fund towards the production of this book.

We also wish to acknowledge and thank the individual donors who gave to the book's production via our 'Sponsor-a-book' campaign.

AUDIO RECORDINGS

The Subtle Art of Caring has been produced with accompanying guided meditations by River Wolton. They are indicated by this image

These can be streamed directly from the web.

Please go to bit.ly/ https://tinyurl.com/TSAoC-audio or https://www.windhorsepublications.com/free-resources/tsaoc-audio/

FOREWORD

The Subtle Art of Caring: A Guide to Sustaining Compassion is an essential and timely contribution to navigating the unprecedented mega challenges destabilizing the world's environmental, political, economic, and social systems. The turmoil of social inequities, climate breakdown, geopolitical conflicts, and sharp political divisions is impacting us all with increasing intensity. We have entered a more threatening world, activating a kaleidoscope of dissonant emotions, which often leaves us overwhelmed and unable to find the ground beneath us or our ability to marshal an effective response.

As we traverse this tumultuous landscape, it is critical that we have truthful, compassionate, and caring companions for support to help us engage the calamitous reality of our times. River Wolton's gentle yet piercing, clear, and doable approach, born of personal experience, deep introspection, and a commitment to social and environmental justice, is just this kind of companion. Page by page, we are uplifted and are reminded of the nourishing potency of kindness, empathy, and the peerless wisdom of the Dharma.

Many of us, reeling from the daily round of apocalyptic news deregulating our nervous systems, have become increasingly susceptible to heightened stress states that trigger cycles of disassociation. We tend to be less self-caring when we don't feel grounded and are dislocated from our core sense of wellbeing. Consequently, our capacity to effectively and positively engage our work, relationships, and the wider world diminishes. The power of River's book is to lovingly gather us back into a simplicity of being, which helps us remember what we so easily forget; to pause, befriend, enjoy, care, let be, and practise sustaining compassion and non-harming.

As we journey into the book's heart, we are encouraged to explore the power and beauty of compassionate living. In a world where spaces for authentic human connection are becoming rarer, we are reminded that compassion is the real currency of life. The Covid-19 pandemic, extreme political division, deepening economic hardship, and the addictive, hollow world of social media have created a fraught world of people atomized in their own, often lonely, silos. Somehow, we must find ways to reclaim a feeling of togetherness.

River's personal stories offer many examples of togetherness, particularly through her activism, like her participation in the Greenham Common Women's Peace Camp. This twenty-year-long anti-nuclear protest surrounding the Royal Air Force base in the UK, housing US cruise missiles, was an extraordinary achievement. This action is one of history's most successful non-violent resistance movements. The example of this often-forgotten heroic effort is particularly inspiring for this moment when we all urgently need to be activists to have any hope of a liveable future.

Drawing from Buddhist teachings, personal experience, and conversations with a diverse range of people, while not shying away from the brutal history of colonialism, *The Subtle Art of Caring* shares examples of everyday acts of compassion, encouraging us to be good ancestors who care for the wellbeing of future generations. In this way, we are offered a path to leave the isolation of our socially conditioned individualism and nurture compassion and fierce love instead.

In her book, River points us to the possibility of cultivating our supple hearts. She developed this skill by realizing that even in the face of great suffering, it is possible to stay grounded and not be consumed by the world's pain. This pivotal Buddhist insight frees us to stand beside suffering without being crushed. We, too, can pivot from pain, despair, and hopelessness to a way of living that can accommodate the 10,000 joys and sorrows while still maintaining a tender, rather than armoured, heart.

Connecting with nature, the significance of community, and cultivating gratitude, wisdom, courage, and a generous spirit doesn't mean we can't also maintain appropriate boundaries for self-care.

Finding this kind of balance, which *The Subtle Art of Caring* shows is possible, is one of life's great achievements.

This wonderful book is a friend, ally, and true guide for living authentically in an acutely uncertain world. Woven through the pages are powerful teachings, evocative stories, exquisite poetry, and supportive heart practices. Taking this journey with River is like leaving a crowded, hot city and instead stepping onto a winding path through a glade of trees through which dappled light reveals a garden filled with scented roses, wildflowers, medicinal herbs, and healing waterfalls. The invitation to take such a journey should not be missed.

Thanissara, Bay Area, California, 9 June 2023

INTRODUCTION

A crisis is too good a chance to waste. There is a gift, as well as dread, in living through these times.

Alastair McIntosh[1]

In August 1981 Sally MacKean and I went to the USSR. We were eighteen, not long out of boarding school. Fuelled by reading Tolstoy, Dostoevsky, and Solzhenitsyn, fascinated by socialism and hungry for adventure, we boarded an Aeroflot plane for Moscow. Soon we discovered we had unwittingly booked our tour behind the Iron Curtain with a travel agent affiliated to the Communist Party of Great Britain, and that our travelling companions were trade-union activists and Party members. Undismayed by our naivety and privilege, they took us under their wing. In train carriages lumbering between Russian cities, we learned there was 'No war but the class war' and how to sing 'The Internationale'. Plied with vodka and greeted with heartfelt speeches by young communists and workers, we were spellbound by the apparent commitment to peace, the statistics on full employment, education, and gender equality. We queued to see Lenin's embalmed body in Red Square, tried to slip away from our long-suffering minder Viktor, nibbled hot *pirozhki* at street stalls, and browsed the tourist shops that Russians were barred from entering.

Some of this book's seeds were planted that summer, in utopian visions of justice and solidarity. As we sang, drank, argued, and drank some more with our newfound communist aunties and uncles, we absorbed their commitment, entranced by how they welcomed our questions. But undercurrents lingered in those Soviet hotel rooms: sorrows drowned in alcohol, guilt's undertow, party lines that brooked no dissent, the hazards of idealism, the pressure to sacrifice oneself on the altar of a just cause, the despair at a ceaseless tide of injustice.

'These are dangerous days', sang Sinéad O'Connor, calling out the racism, police brutality, and social inequality of Thatcher's Britain.[2] The 1980s also witnessed the AIDS pandemic, and a menacing turn in the Cold War. The deadly double-act of Margaret Thatcher and Ronald Reagan brought nuclear-armed cruise missiles to RAF Greenham Common. In preparation for conflict, mobile missile launchers were transported to secret locations, but were tracked and often brought to a standstill by protestors. Gravitating to feminist and peace activism, I demonstrated at Greenham Women's Peace Camp, Embraced the Base, and marched with CND.

After leaving university I worked with people with multiple disabilities, then trained as a social worker and psychotherapist. Several years later I burned out. Working at a rape and sexual-abuse

counselling centre, I realized I no longer saw people as people: there was only the reality of gender-based violence, all men were actual or potential perpetrators, all women survivors. I sought answers in lesbian separatism, vitalized by radical feminism, endeavouring to create a new world and destroy the white-supremacist hetero-patriarchy, but unable to understand how I had internalized it.

Encounters with Buddhism provoked rage. I wanted inner and outer peace, but was mistrustful of the Dharma's patriarchal roots and misogynist leanings, and the emotional repression it seemed to advocate. Marx's famous dictum coloured my suspicions: religion is the opium of the masses. I explored different meditation traditions but often felt alienated and sceptical. Reading *A Path with Heart* by Jack Kornfield, recommended during my psychotherapy training, revealed an approach informed by psychology and social justice, and a lineage of socially engaged teachers, including Thich Nhat Hanh and Joanna Macy. On silent retreats I touched into the delight of relinquishing assumptions. No less moved to care and challenge injustice, I glimpsed how fixed opinions obstruct freedom, and that a space between impulse and reactivity could be cultivated in the service of clarity. Slowly I began to understand what underpinned these compulsions, and the value of an embodied practice, realizing that non-harm and compassion needed to be congruent in means and ends, and to be practised towards all beings including myself.

Working as a creative-writing facilitator, initially inspired by Natalie Goldberg's Zen writing-practice method, means I have witnessed hundreds of people find new perspectives on experience through crafting it into words and images. In schools, public libraries, care homes, mental-health settings, with looked-after teenagers, and in carers' support groups I have seen the transformative power of creativity. Art does not put food in hungry mouths, but it does have the potential to reveal unheard or silenced stories, to reconnect us with shared humanity, and to help us look further than immediate preoccupations. The poet and rabbi Mónica Gomery reflects:

> I think of creative process as a spiritual practice, and in both art-making and ritual it can serve us to be non-judgmental and curious toward ourselves, to let ourselves be transformed by what we discover in these generative forms. Poetry and prayer are both also somatic practices rooted in the breath and body.[3]

In spring 2003 millions marched again for peace as the US, UK, and allies prepared to invade Iraq. Shock at seeing bombs falling on Baghdad gave way to despair. Standing in peace vigils I met Iraqi Kurds persecuted by the regime and relieved to see Saddam Hussein toppled. Waking up to the way thousands of asylum seekers were being dispersed by the Home Office to cities in northern England, I became involved with refugee support, witnessing the racism and xenophobia embedded in the asylum and immigration system, as well as the courage and resilience of those who resist and survive it. In these years, I also became aware of a disruptive creativity and humour flavouring non-violent direct action: the Clandestine Insurgent Rebel Clown Army, Rhythms of Resistance, the Street Choir movement, and more. At the Faslane 365 blockade in 2006, there were new levels of organization, affinity groups, and legal support needed for effective protest.

Twenty years on from the Second Gulf War, a familiar horror returns as I read George Monbiot's words:

> With the exception of all-out nuclear war, all the most important issues that confront us are environmental. None of our hopes, none of our dreams, none of our plans and expectations can survive the loss of a habitable planet. And there is scarcely an Earth system that is not now threatened with collapse.[4]

Crisis and care

The Anthropocene will be a narrow geological layer but will testify to mass extinction caused by human activity. Population growth, climate change, and the destruction of ecosystems may, in the next decades, create shortages of food and natural resources, pressure on habitable and cultivatable land, the displacement and forced migration of millions. The 2020s must be a period of rapid mitigation and adaptation to safeguard humanity from the worst harms. Without immediate, large-scale reductions in greenhouse-gas emissions, limiting warming to 1.5° or even 2° will be beyond reach.[5] Whether humans survive or not, our species is extinguishing many others, and impacting life not just on this planet but even beyond. Millions of space-debris particles now orbit Earth, and their presence is an increasing threat to space missions, satellites, and the International Space Station. In total, 400,000 pounds of debris have been left on the moon, including ninety-six bags of human waste.[6]

In the face of climate collapse, threats to global security from Russia's invasion of Ukraine, and escalating social inequities, horrified anxiety seems an appropriate response. As with any form of fear, our nervous systems become dysregulated, defaulting to survival patterns of fight, flight, freeze, collapse, and follow – the latter exemplified by a gravitation towards charismatic political and spiritual leaders, and social-media influencers. We shrink from feeling overwhelmed, or ricochet between denial and alarm, transfixed by screens that bring immediate, constant access to the scale of suffering, but leave us disempowered. Researchers have found, for example, that people with extensive media exposure to the Boston Marathon bombings had higher levels of acute stress than those directly affected by the attack.[7]

We may care deeply, but, when doom-scrolling removes us from the immediacy of crisis, we lose agency, and any action seems inadequate and futile. Some describe this as compassion fatigue; Zen abbot and medical anthropologist Roshi Joan Halifax reframes it as empathic distress, where we are called to our edges, resonating with pain but unable to stabilize ourselves.[8] 'We can learn', she writes, 'from these dangerous territories. Edges are places where opposites meet. Where fear meets courage and suffering meets freedom.'[9]

There are immense disparities in these interrelated social, racial, ecological crises. Nations in the Global North are responsible for 92 per cent of excess CO_2 emissions.[10] Their economic growth is founded on the exploitation of countries in the Global South, who now bear the brunt of climate destabilization, and have less power in international climate negotiations. These crises also have different impacts depending, for example, on racialized identities and age. People of colour in the US are disproportionately affected by, and more concerned about, climate change than white people.[11] A study of 10,000 children and young people in ten countries chosen to reflect a range of cultures, incomes, and climate vulnerabilities showed high levels of climate anxiety; 75 per cent said they think the future is frightening, and 45 per cent said their feelings about climate change negatively affected their daily functioning.[12]

Pressures are intensifying on social-care systems, as long-term impacts of Covid-19 and climate-related pressures on health take hold. There is secondary or vicarious trauma from witnessing pain that can't be alleviated, as well as the moral injury sustained by frontline workers rendered unable to provide care in appropriate ways because of systemic failures. Increasing life expectancy means more people need care, and more are caregivers. Those giving personal care, those who bathe and dress, who feed and wipe, are disproportionately likely to be women, working-class, black and brown people and people of colour, and to be paid the least.[13] 'The best kind of care is like sunshine', writes a ninety-year-old woman living in a care home.[14] When we are at our most vulnerable, we know what it feels like, and how important it is, to be well cared for. Increasing numbers (6.5 million in the UK) provide unpaid care and support to a family member, friend, or neighbour who is disabled or has an illness or long-term health condition.[15] Many carers face the dual responsibility of caring for elderly relatives as well as their own children, and research from Germany reveals how Covid magnified parental burnout and overwhelming exhaustion, particularly for mothers.[16]

A carer describes their isolation:

Caring has a life of its own,
it lifts invisible weights
in a room with fog seeping in,
and a half-frozen fish pie.[17]

No one is immune from illness, ageing, and dying. And yet we collectively denigrate and deny these states, as well as those who attend to and alleviate them.

Such crises require large-scale state allocation of resources, as well as the profound social change and shifts in actions, practices, and consciousness that Joanna Macy calls 'The Great Turning'.[18] We need to learn how to look after each other and the world around us, in ways that are equitable, sustainable in the long term, and versatile enough to respond to sudden shocks as well as chronic calamities. Poet and activist Tchiyiwe Chihana, who works on environmental and social-justice issues in the media, arts, and culture, particularly with women of African heritage, and campaigns for a universal basic income, speaks of the pressures:

> The narrative of the status quo is informed by mainstream media and protected by institutions, and there's constant burnout on the frontline in fighting for everyday survival; the system is not sustainable, it's a vicious cycle. That's why we need to fight for systems change, bringing in people who can look at it from a possibility-oriented perspective, taking it where it needs to go.[19]

Caring activity and response take multiple forms: for some, the immediacy of parenting, being a carer, or working in a caring profession; for others, engaging in volunteering, organizing, social justice. The approach of this book is to see care in its broadest sense, defining activism as any action of service, generosity, or change-making.

Beautiful resistance

In 2014 I was one of 130 writers and climate scientists brought together by the charity TippingPoint for the 'Weatherfronts: Climate Change and the Stories We Tell' conference. Among the presentations, Professor Chris Rapley showed a speeded-up version of ocean-surface temperature change. We held our breath as the decades passed and colours on the screen shifted from blue to green to yellow, orange, then deep red. He entreated us to keep climate in the foreground of our work. 'ClimateCultures – Creative Conversations for the Anthropocene', a website curated by Mark Goldthorpe, is an outcome of the conference, one of many gathering points for artists exploring the power of an environmental imagination to develop a sense of agency.[20]

Olivia Laing, celebrating art as a force of resistance and repair, writes:

> We're so often told that art can't really change anything. But I think it can. It shapes our ethical landscapes; it opens us to the interior lives of others. It is a training ground for possibility. It makes plain inequalities, and it offers other ways of living.[21]

A review of the pathways through which climate change interacts with mental and physical health and wellbeing concludes that, while the relationships are complex, strong psychological responses can be adaptive:[22]

> Recognising that emotions are often what lead people to act, it is possible that feelings of ecological anxiety and grief, although uncomfortable, are in fact the crucible through which humanity must pass to harness the energy and conviction that are needed for the lifesaving changes now required.[23]

Emergency and adaptation have the potential to reawaken capacities used by humans for millennia to survive and thrive, including art that celebrates, mourns, and rebels. Creativity can flourish in the most anguished circumstances. The Alrowwad Culture and Arts project in Aida refugee camp, Bethlehem, celebrates a 'Beautiful Resistance' against Israeli occupation, empowering children, youth, and women through creative and non-violent means. Alrowwad aims to be one of

the premier institutions for visual and performing arts in Palestine, seeing every individual as a change-maker. 'We do not have the luxury of despair,' says its founder Dr Abdelfattah Abusrour, 'we don't wait for miracles to happen, we provoke them.'[24]

In NGOs and humanitarian organizations burnout is endemic, but skilful responses are germinating. In grassroots communities, disruption is a wellspring for regenerative action. There is potential, increasingly realized, to understand the challenges with clarity, and yet turn also to the capacities that can arise in the face of suffering: creativity, courage, confidence, generosity. As health and social-care systems face collapse, calls grow for a systemic shift in how people at the frontlines of care are valued, and how social inequality must be radically transformed.

The spread of mindfulness-based applications in the last thirty years has mainstreamed contemplative practices that originate in the Buddhist tradition, and a growing movement explores the potential of mindfulness in creating sustainable and just societies. Research by The Mindfulness Initiative found that climate change is both the result of an inner crisis of disconnection, and a cause of anxiety and overwhelm that leads to further disconnection.[25] This vicious cycle triggers denial, and deterioration of wellbeing and psychological resilience, leading in turn to consumerism and overconsumption that create greater ecological destruction. Evidence shows that mindfulness and compassion are central to integrative new approaches in a decade when the IPCC has declared Code Red for humanity.

Practices that build somatic and psychological resilience and find a middle way between denial and alarm include Earth Vigils or Climate Vigils, where people of all faiths and no faith bear silent witness in public, acknowledging frustration, fear, and grief, and remembering that those who have done least to cause these emergencies are suffering their worst effects.[26] Another example is The Resilience Project UK, a youth-led movement fostering communities of collective care, drawing on the latest insights from psychology and neuroscience, and combining action, rest, and joy.[27]

Faith groups are collaborating with campaigners: Alaa' Al-Samarrai, from Islamic Relief UK, writes in a blogpost for the pressure group Hope for the Future:

Our mosques are uniquely placed institutions which can make significant strides in the fight for our climate, and community leaders have already demonstrated great leadership in engaging and advocating for local climate action. Working with other faith communities, we can increase the impact and extend our message, drawing on our shared values and aspirations for the future of our planet.[28]

Yanai Postelnik (meditation teacher and activist interviewed in Chapter 5) touches on the potential for action and contemplative practice to inform each other: 'Bringing these together expresses an understanding that the inner work and the outer work aren't separate from each other.'

The *Dhammapada*, a well-known Buddhist text, describes the tendencies of an untrained mind:

The restless, agitated mind,
    Hard to protect, hard to control ...

Like a fish out of water,
    Thrown on dry ground,
This mind thrashes about,
    Trying to escape Mara's command.

> The mind, hard to control,
>   Flighty – alighting where it wishes –
> One does well to tame.
>   The disciplined mind brings happiness.[29]

Restlessness and agitation may seem like soundly appropriate responses to threat, but, when they take up residence in the driving seat of awareness, they assume the solidity of facts and become the only lens through which everything is viewed. When we are pulled in one direction or another by unreliable compulsions, compass directions are obscured, and clarity blurred. The *Dhammapada* speaks of taming and discipline; the development of mindful awareness also needs tenderness and patience, a kindly discipline that leans into enquiry and learning rather than rigidity. Mindfulness without a basis in non-harming means the mind tends to be occupied with regret. Without a foundation of morality, meditation is 'like trying to row a boat across a river, exerting a lot of effort in the process, but never untying the rope from the dock. It doesn't go anywhere.'[30] And an ethics of non-harm entails the development of kindness and compassion.

Compassion and its companions

Humans for Abundance (H4A), a social enterprise engaged in climate restoration in Ecuador, expresses the need to reframe language:

> The messaging (used in the rhetoric of climate crisis) almost unilaterally suggests a scarcity mindset. Scarcity of time, resources, nature, political capital, and people who care. It's not that these claims are untrue... While H4A acknowledges the realities of climate change and its social implications, they bring something new to the table – a frame of abundance. An abundance of ideas, people, creativity, and the will to make a change.[31]

Even the vocabulary we choose can alter perception. Susie Dent argues that the English language tends to retain the negative versions of words but not their positive counterparts, for example 'respair', last recorded in 1525, meaning fresh hope, a recovery from despair.[32] This book

aspires to offer both respair and a radical reframing. Through a collage of reflections, conversations, and creative explorations, the intention is to show that the stories we tell, and how we tell them, can help navigate vulnerability and existential threats. It attempts to gather resources that move against the stream of twenty-first-century memes: the myth of eternal economic growth, the imperative of individualism and self-improvement, the pull to deny embodiment. By drawing attention to inalienable and renewable capacities, it flies in the face of late capitalism's hyperconsumerism and broken-record tale of scarcity and urgency: 'Buy now while stocks last!'

Can we shift possibilities by telling a different story that subverts habits of extraction and depletion? In *Braiding Sweetgrass: Indigenous Wisdom, Scientific Knowledge, and the Teachings of Plants*, Robin Wall Kimmerer highlights a reciprocity that goes beyond sustainability. Professor of Environmental Biology and member of the Citizen Potawatomi Nation, she describes her work as 'an intertwining of science, spirit, and story'.[33] Let's imagine, she writes, that we have the inherent ability and sense of responsibility to sustain the Earth, just as we are sustained by her.

The framework of immeasurable capacities or *brahma-viharas* that is a central part of Buddhist philosophy responds directly to these questions. Kindness (*metta*), compassion (*karuna* or *anukampa*), joy (*mudita*), and equanimity (*upekkha*) are akin to qualities valued by both secular and faith-based approaches. They are multidimensional: as contemplation subjects, relational practices, therapeutic tools, and pathways of absorption and insight. A poem by Longchenpa, a fourteenth-century Tibetan writer and teacher, describes how they intersect:

Out of the soil of friendliness
Grows the beautiful bloom of compassion
Watered by the tears of joy
Sheltered beneath the cool shade of the tree
    of equanimity[34]

These images reflect the premise that, without the support of its companions, compassion – the capacity to care and respond – will not survive and thrive. Like other expressions of life, it requires certain conditions to flower. Without the nourishment and protection of friendliness, joy, and equanimity, it distorts into its near and far enemies: pity, overwhelm, disconnection, cruelty, and burnout.

'Brahma-vihara' has varied translations in English: 'boundless heart', 'divine abode', 'infinite mind', 'heavenly realm'. An origin story tells of monastics who identified a jungle grove eminently suitable for sustained meditation practice, and settled in for a three-month retreat. The tree deities living in the grove with their families were, however, alarmed and displaced by the sudden arrival of a large crowd, and, uncertain how long the visitors would stay, they reacted by unleashing terrifying sounds and smells. Hurrying back to the Buddha, the practitioners were told to return to the forest, to recite the *Metta Sutta* on boundless loving-kindness, and to 'rejoice, and pursue, develop and cultivate this meditation subject'.[35] Filled with 'rapture and joy' that the monks wished them well, the tree deities warmly welcomed them back.[36] The fable shows how terror can be transformed through the development of these unconditional capacities. It reflects the ways, common to all places and times, in which fear can be met and changed by love.

The brahma-viharas originate in a pre-Buddhist concept, one to which the Buddhist tradition gave its own interpretation. In the *Tevijja Sutta* the Buddha advises young Brahmins eager to know the quickest way to heaven. Not through perfecting rituals or memorizing sacred texts, he counsels, but through a path of harmlessness and meditation, cultivating these four heavenly realms to suffuse the world with heart-liberating benevolence.[37]

Who cares?

'Upekkha' or 'equanimity', pictured in Longchenpa's poem as a tree's cool shade, also translates as 'steadiness', 'balance', or 'inclusiveness'. It is associated with cooling the fires of greed, hatred, and delusion, and the teachings of not-self, dependent arising, and emptiness. Often misunderstood – now as in ancient India – as nihilistic, in many respects these teachings are pragmatic ones pointing towards the freedom of clear knowing and seeing. When accused of nihilism, the Buddha responded:

> I have been falsely misrepresented as being what I am not, and saying what I do not say. In the past, as today, what I describe is suffering [*dukkha*] and the cessation of suffering [*nirodha*].[38]

The medicine for the suffering of burnout, empathic distress, and secondary trauma is the same as for all forms of dukkha: the tasks of embracing and fully knowing it, understanding its origin, and cultivating a path that leads to its ending. Insight into dukkha is a gateway to a lighter, more creative perception of self. The trajectory of this book points towards the realization that fixed identities – such as 'the one who cares', 'the one who should care more', or 'the one who can never do enough' – are forms of suffering, constricting and undermining the capacity for compassion.

Compassion itself is impermanent. The verb 'to sustain' implies continuity and endurance, but compassion comes and goes, like all conditioned phenomena. Sustainable compassion is a contradiction in terms; a belief that it can be maintained indefinitely without faltering is one of the things that gets in the way. Yet cultivating compassion can become a lifelong art and craft, sustaining us as we move back and forth in the dance of sustaining it. And, as Yanai Postelnik affirms in Chapter 5, it is 'something the heart can rest on, even in the most terrible of circumstances'.[39]

Ways in

Inspired by Longchenpa's poem, and by Buddhism's primary texts, many of which brim with similes and metaphors, I have used creative licence to weave poetry into the text. The brahma-viharas are dwelling places; in early Pali and Sanskrit texts 'vihara' meant 'a living space', and later came to mean 'monastic quarters'. I've taken a non-linear approach to investigating their facets and nuances, with the intention of creating images of welcoming hearths, where we can stay awhile, warm ourselves at their firesides, rest, take nourishment, and engage in conversation and creativity. Emma Burleigh's watercolours mirror this and add the wonderful dimension of visual imagery, another gateway into these abodes.

I've altered the traditional order of the brahma-viharas, placing joy before compassion, and beginning with a chapter on pausing, rest, and embodiment, to emphasize antidotes to depletion. Each of the brahma-viharas can be a doorway into the others. Longchenpa's poem begins with the ground of metta, but, for some, equanimity is the entryway; for others, as Kareem Ghandour says in Chapter 3, 'joy is like the first step, an easy springboard.'[40]

Awakening is a collective endeavour, and good friendship, companionship, or comradeship – as the Buddha reminds his cousin Ananda – is not half but the whole of the path.[41] Early in the project I realized the need to talk to people on the frontlines of inner and outer action and activism, and I have woven these conversations into the book, drawing on this collective body of wisdom. These insights and perspectives highlight the importance of community, and the need for a collaborative response to emergency. In quoting the words and experiences of practitioners, friends, and teachers, I have followed the terms and forms with which they self-describe, for example as Black or black, BIPOC or person of colour.

I have mixed Pali terms with English translations. 'Metta', often translated as 'loving-kindness', is not fully conveyed by either 'love' or 'kindness'. We are yoked to the conventions and pragmatism of language, but words fall short when they try to capture experience, particularly the embodied awareness of capacities described as boundless. Words are only signs that approximately translate concepts, and renditions of 2,000-year-old texts are contingent on temporal and cultural context. Pali is the language, related to Sanskrit, in which early discourses were written down around 300 years after the Buddha's death, and is thought to be akin to the language spoken by the Buddha, although, in the oral tradition that preserved the teachings, other voices, dialects, and languages are blended. The intention in using Pali or Sanskrit words is not to mystify, but to signal the value of finding one's own embodied translations through direct experience.

Although the reflections offered here are inspired by Buddhist practice, no specific beliefs are required to engage with them. Philosophies are not necessarily true or useful because they are ancient or described by others as wise. The Dharma (teachings of the Buddhist tradition) invites you to come and find out for yourself, through direct experience, what makes a difference. The only way we discern this is through trial and error, through venturing, failing, and trying again, discovering, mainly via encountering obstacles, what brings confidence and leads onwards. Resources at the end of the book include recollections for daily practice that can help reorientate towards harmlessness and compassion in the midst of life.

Some of the explorations may open painful or traumatic memories of times when you have suffered or witnessed suffering. Take care of yourself and pull back when needed. Some sections touch quite briefly on areas that are long-term, life-long investigations, and the book is not a substitute for the one-to-one support of a mentor, counsellor, or therapist.

The 'creative exploration' sections, and Emma's images, can be used as starting points for your own journeys with compassion and its companions. The word 'creative' can be off-putting and induce pressure to produce something; please know that anything goes. The Pali word *bhavana*, often rendered as 'meditation', can also be translated as 'bringing into being'. This points to a view of contemplative practice as an inherently creative activity either generating something new or uncovering what is innate. Pause and drop the reflections into awareness, see what happens inwardly, or respond outwardly through writing, imagining, drawing, singing, visualizing, moving, playing, having a conversation... and much more. Find a way to incorporate them into

things you're already doing, or use them to try something new. The recordings of guided meditations that accompany the book can also be used as starting points.

The brahma-viharas are inner resources, birthrights innate to the human condition, able to be cultivated and developed, and rooted in the challenges of our ordinary, extraordinary, and often messy human experience. They require no preparation, equipment, or conditions. In the words of Sufi poet Jalal al-Din Rumi, 'The door is round and open / Don't go back to sleep.'[42] Come in just as you are and know that you are wholeheartedly welcome.

Chapter 1
PAUSING

In the face of the intensifying compulsion of production and performance, finding a way to make a different, playful use of life is a political task. Life regains its playful element when it relates to itself instead of subordinating itself to an external purpose. What must be won back is contemplative rest. If our life is deprived of all its contemplative elements, we become suffocated by our own activity.

Byung-Chul Han[43]

The pleasure and pain of pausing

Contemplative practices such as mindfulness, meditation, or prayer gift us a pause from life's momentum. A respite from scrolling and clicking. Temporary rest from the insatiable pull to get away from it all, to reach towards an ever-receding horizon. 'Learn to meditate so you can pause for a bit' is a flimsy advert, but it can be a radical proposition and harder to do than we imagine. Slowing down and stopping go against the stream of acquiring, gratifying, and getting distracted, against the compulsion to keep reassuring ourselves that we are occupied and thus worthwhile.

Even when we do stop, once we return to busyness and momentum builds again, we may soon forget any benefits that stopping brought, and need to be reminded many times. Hence the term 'practice': a repeated activity that hones a skill and functions to remind us of a chosen direction. For those of us who struggle to regulate ourselves in relation to commitments, it can take a long time, a lot of practice, to learn to slow down and settle. And even if we don't feel overcommitted, there can still be an inner busyness and agitation.

For some, rest is not a choice, but a non-negotiable long-term condition enforced, for example, by long Covid, ME, chronic fatigue, illness, or disability. Whether disabled or able-bodied, we have a relationship to pausing and stopping, both internalized and externalized in collective judgements about activity, productivity, and worth, reflected in the ableism and stigma engrained in social attitudes. When the body is apparently at rest, the mind can still be ceaselessly in motion, busy and proliferating. In this chapter, pausing and resting refer as much, if not more, to the mind's activity as to the body's.

When we consider pausing, there may be conscious or unconscious views that it is self-indulgent and a waste of time. Being able to stop and do nothing can seem a privilege and a luxury. Many have no choice but to labour, with merciless demands and little time for rest. Denying oneself the possibility of pausing, however, does not improve the quality of others' lives. Unhooking from compulsive busyness and pressure is a form of first aid, a step towards the art of long-term sustainability.

Zohar Lavie and Nathan Glyde bring unique perspectives to the power and practice of stopping. Co-founders of SanghaSeva, they lead retreats in India, Palestine, Israel, the UK, and Europe, bringing together meditation, engaged caring, and activism.[44]

My first impression of Zohar was the way she embodied pausing. It would be some years before I spoke to her, and then the fire in her eyes and her animated speech left no doubts about her energy and fierce commitment. But, as we gardened silently together on a meditation-in-action retreat, replanting a school garden, I was impressed by how carefully she worked. Hundreds of flower bulbs lay waiting beside us, the beds were thick with weeds, but here was a woman who seemed immune to urgency. My pace slowed and habitual work modes receded as I absorbed this wordless teaching.

I met Nathan as a fellow meditator on a month-long silent retreat – we passed each other in the corridors, washed saucepans in the kitchen, but didn't speak. I noticed his capacity for steadiness, how he stood motionless outside, facing the sun as it rose or set. Some years later, when I understood the depth of his care and the lightness of his humour, I would feel both respect and surprise to see him resting in an olive tree's shade while others worked around him. I admired the courage to lay cares aside, and wondered if I'd have the nerve to ignore the tide of urgent tasks.

Zohar explains how they developed a balance between engaged caring and time to stop. Much of their learning took place through working retreats that offer massage and personal care to older people at a community in Maharashtra, India. Anandwan, established in 1949 by Baba Amte, environmentalist and social reformer known as 'the modern Gandhi', gives marginalized people affected by leprosy a dignified life through self-reliance and a sense of belonging. It has expanded into a large-scale project providing health care, education, and employment.[45]

Our original vision (which reflects our personalities) was: 'We're going to get in there and *Do Do Do!*' We had set aside time for meditation, but the focus was on engagement. Rushing from meditation to work to meal, we realized the need to build in spaces for deepening and resourcing, and the importance of unscheduled time. It's counterintuitive that we need that breathing space. Just as we need both the out-breath and the in-breath to stay alive, we need the space between things for them to take root and evolve.

CREATIVE EXPLORATION

Stop now. Put everything aside for a few moments. Close your eyes or keep them open but unfocused. Take a few conscious breaths, some of the 20,000 you will breathe today. Notice the faint pause between in-breath and out-breath, and a more discernible pause between out- and in-breath. Notice how your body expands slightly as you inhale, and releases as you exhale. Tune in to life's momentum as it moves through you. You might become aware of your pulse or heartbeat. Perhaps restlessness, tiredness, impatience, a hankering, some calm, or irritation. Likely you'll start to notice that thoughts flit about like butterflies or bees, meandering or homing in on the past or future.

Pausing, even for a moment, reveals the astonishing energy of internal preoccupations, even when external activity has stopped. This can be shocking, whether we are seeing it for the first time or the thousandth. It's not helped by the ways in which meditation and mindfulness are often advertised: people sitting quietly, looking relaxed and serene. Becoming aware of what happens when we pause or stop disrupts an underlying assumption that we are in control of our thoughts. Unfortunately, we often believe that our preoccupied mind is a shameful personal failing, and something to be denied or rejected.

When we're forced out of our usual activities, as in Covid lockdowns, it can be both frightening and liberating. We are displaced from routines, and realize more clearly that what we do, and how we perform, can define and limit us. Other avenues and creative perspectives open up.

Nathan describes what can unfold in taking time to stop:

There's a human hunger for results and a hunger to keep feeding the mind. If, for example, on the Being Peace retreats we said: 'We've done a lot of olive picking, now we're going to have a day off', people might think, 'I'll do some sight-seeing.' So we call them silent days rather than days off, and the intention is to go to places inside, a sight-seeing of the heart. We support that urge for hunger inwardly, and start to have the digestion processes, getting in tune with what we really want and reflecting on what's been happening. Through that prism we see our motivations more clearly, how much greed and aversion are lingering, and how much harm we might be causing to ourselves and others. We see ways we can disentangle from them, and we find a certain freedom within experience that also liberates us to be in the world.

Time and care

When we are looking after children time slows, but their energy is limitless. In a toddler's company, the hours elongate. The clock almost stops. By mid-morning we've built cities, had a snack, baked biscuits, travelled on an imaginary horse to Spain and Africa, read ten books, been to the playground. Pushing the swing to shouts of 'Higher, higher!', I try to feel my feet on the ground. Tiredness mixes with the tenderness of having no energy other than to be present and respond to immediate needs. Unlike parents, I don't know the long-term reality of this exhaustion, but in this moment I have forgotten I ever wrote books, chaired a meeting, made life decisions, found time to brush my teeth. All other selves dematerialize. Time is a concept, subjective and malleable.

In busy moments, time speeds up. But – even if we understand the paradoxical effect of having more time when we slow down – there is a fear that in pausing we'll achieve less, or grind to a halt.

Zohar picks up this theme:

When we pause we can come into the body, with the heart and mind, with awareness, attention, and spaciousness. That recharges the batteries quickly and more fully than just napping or reading a book. It regenerates energy and supports re-engagement with tasks.

The proof is in the difference between what people look like at the beginning and the end of a meditation day. The change from being drained to the sense of deep ease. People come on a meditation-in-action retreat and expect to be doing and giving all the time, so it's sometimes difficult to stop. But then they see that's the way we should be living, with this balance.

CREATIVE EXPLORATION

How do you experience time?

What or who helps you pause?

Experiment with not responding immediately to the next demand, message, or email. What do you notice?

Guilt and shame

If only, I hear you say. If only I could take time out, even for a moment. If the weekend would come sooner, if demands would decrease, if work wasn't crazy, if my kids or elders would stop needing things. If only I could be certain that, once I stopped, I'd find the energy to start again.

Without ignoring the real pressures to make ends meet and put food on the table, it's also possible to examine how habit patterns, individual and collective, rule our interactions with work, rest, and play. The history of timekeeping illuminates a centuries-old push-and-pull relationship with productivity, purpose, and ease. A sundial,taken as a trophy of war from Catania, is believed to be one of the first public clocks. It was installed in Rome in 263 BCE and led to a proliferation of sundials. The comedic playwright Plautus gave this speech to one of his characters:

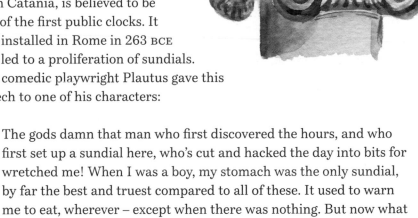

> The gods damn that man who first discovered the hours, and who first set up a sundial here, who's cut and hacked the day into bits for wretched me! When I was a boy, my stomach was the only sundial, by far the best and truest compared to all of these. It used to warn me to eat, wherever – except when there was nothing. But now what there is, isn't eaten unless the sun says so. In fact town's so stuffed with sundials that most people crawl along, shrivelled up with hunger.[46]

Guilt and shame can function like the dictatorial sundials of consciousness, impelling us to do, get, justify. Not to eat or rest unless they say so. To dance to their tunes, which are primarily songs of lack and unworthiness, rooted in cultural or religious work ethics, or a capitalist imperative to produce and be purposeful. Zohar summarizes a common question, and offers a response:

'How can I take this time for me when there's so much work to be done?'

One response is seeing *myself* as part of the totality of life. To see that caring for myself is part of caring for the planet. Being able to hold the magnitude of the work that is needed, and to feel myself as part of that, but that it's not only on my shoulders. By looking after this body, heart, and mind, I'm making myself *more* available rather than less. This goes against conditioning and habits, and it's something we learn over time. We become more resilient, more able to step in when it's needed. It doesn't have to be through meditation – for some people that's not the avenue – it can be through something else that nourishes.

Nathan adds:

Almost everyone I know is overtired, overstretched, and has a cultural sense that by 'doing' they will deserve freedom, rest, and rejuvenation, but these will be forever out of reach. Meditation offers a very subtle doing, the disentangling of the Dharma. It's a way of doing that ends up with us doing less, but it's not a non-doing. It's not indifference to the way things are. Can I do a little less, let my shoulders down, let my belly out, let my mind empty for a moment? ... Then I'm in a moment of calm and I don't need to fill it with something else.

CREATIVE EXPLORATION

Pause and bring awareness to your hands and arms. Scan through the things that these limbs have done today. Invite some out-breaths to soften and loosen the back of your neck, shoulders, and shoulder blades, arms, elbows, wrists, hands, palms, fingers.

How long does pausing last before the thought: 'That's enough now, better get on with the day'?

Radical rest

When we begin to listen to our bodies, the deep geological layers of tiredness and exhaustion may surface, strata that have not been visible or tangible until now.

The Nap Ministry is a pioneer movement 'seeded within the soils of Black radical thought, somatics, Afrofuturism, womanism, and liberation theology'.[47] Founded in 2016 by artist, theologian, and Nap Bishop Tricia Hersey, the Ministry celebrates the liberating power of naps through performance art, site-specific installations, and community organizing. Tricia Hersey's book *Rest Is Resistance* champions rest as reparation, and as a radical tool for healing, naming sleep deprivation as a racial, environmental, and social-justice issue, and sleep as a necessary disruptor of capitalism and white supremacy.[48]

The call to rest manifests in many places. Artist Rahima Gambo began the work *A Rest Guide for a Tired Nigerian Artist* as an experimental documentary diary during pandemic lockdowns and a recession that tagged artistic work as non-essential.[49] In a sequence of guidebooks, she asks other artists for their advice on how to find peace in a troubled world. Their responses are playful, thought-provoking, and direct, including Amanda Iheme's beautifully succinct: 'Number Five: stop working and go outside.'[50]

I recognize that the privileges afforded by whiteness and social class partly insulate me from the imperatives of racialized capitalist work ethics. When they see me downing tools to take a weekday walk, the ghosts of my Presbyterian forebears murmur disapprovingly, but the identity-based bias of the social gaze affords me more freedom to be at leisure, to be a *flâneuse*, a *dilettante*. An attitude to the right to rest is often bound up with racial, class, caste, ableist, and gender conditioning.

Permissions to rest can take many forms. I listen to Handel's *Messiah*, and my heart lifts as a soaring soprano voice sings these words from the Gospel of Matthew: 'Come unto me, all ye that labour and are heavy laden, and ye shall find rest unto your souls.' Rest. The sweetness and welcome of it. Can action incorporate it?

In the eighth century CE the Indian monk Shantideva composed *A Guide to the Bodhisattva's Way of Life*, an invocation of altruism and compassionate action:

May I be a protector for those without one,
A guide for all travellers on the way;
May I be a bridge, a boat and a ship
For all who wish to cross (the water). ...

Just like space
And the great elements such as earth,
May I always support the lives
Of all the boundless creatures.

And until they pass away from pain,
May I also be the source of life
For all the realms of varied beings
That reach unto the ends of space.[51]

The poem emphasizes development of alertness, conscientiousness, patience, enthusiasm, meditation, and wisdom. If this list sounds exhausting, it's good to know that, in the chapter on enthusiasm, rest also gets a mention:

The supports when working for the sake of living beings
Are aspiration, steadfastness, joy and rest. ...

When my strength declines, I should leave whatever I am doing
In order to be able to continue with it later.
Having done something well, I should put it aside
With the wish (to accomplish) what will follow.[52]

Shantideva (who may have been one person or a group of people) is said to have infuriated fellow monastics with their laziness, apparently only interested in food and sleep. When challenged they leapt into action and recited the whole poem by heart. Who knows what may be gestating when we lie fallow?

CREATIVE EXPLORATION

What are your beliefs about rest?

Who and what are your inspirations for rest?

What images, songs, poems, or talismans remind you of the power of rest?

Being bodies

Our bodies and the sense organs they house (eyes, ears, nose, mouth, skin, and mind) are the primary interface with everything we meet – pleasant, unpleasant, and neutral, the lovely, unlovely, extraordinary, and ordinary. Mindfulness of body is the first foundation of mindfulness, tuning us little by little towards becoming more fully embodied. In the *Satipatthana Sutta*, the discourse from which mindfulness-based applications and programmes originate, mindfulness of the body begins with knowing – fully knowing – the in-breath and out-breath just as they are, without the need to alter or judge. It continues with being aware of walking, standing, sitting, lying down, moving forward, and returning, looking this way or that, bending, stretching, eating, drinking, swallowing, urinating, defecating. Nothing is left out. Also included is awareness of internal organs, and how the elements of earth, water, fire, and air manifest in embodiment, and of how the body, this body too, like all bodies, dies and decays.

Nathan reflects on the tendency towards disembodiment:

The mind travels off in space and time, and the body's left behind saying 'Hello! Anyone going to incorporate me?'

Twenty-first-century psychology is developing an increasingly refined understanding of how the body remembers hurt and trauma, how it 'keeps the score'.[53] The fields of trauma-sensitive mindfulness[54] and somatic psychology[55] offer guidance for compassionately exploring embodiment, and for encountering what might show up as this exploration deepens. Bodies can house the imprint of trauma, intergenerational and present-day, including the impact of being marginalized, ranked, or rendered invisible because of gender identity, racialized identity, age, size and shape, disability, neuro-diversity, culture, class, caste, state of health, and many other conditions.

Whether or not we have experienced direct or indirect trauma, all of us know pain, loss, and sudden change; we have been impacted by the 'slings and arrows' of life, by 'the heart-ache and the thousand natural shocks / that flesh is heir to'.[56]

When we slow down and turn towards felt experience in its entirety, sensations, images, and memories that are hard to bear may surface. It is part of our intelligence to store away, repress, or forget, in order to survive as intactly as we can. When painful thought patterns or physical sensations arise, a delicate, essential pathway of care can open.

The terms 'dysregulation' and 'regulation' refer to the ways by which we have learned to cope, or not, with situations that are overwhelming or unpredictable. Sometimes these strategies, and the pain that they've evolved with, come to the fore when we have more time and space, and when we engage in contemplative practice. It's important to remember that we can introduce just a small amount of hurt into a much larger space of kindly awareness, and that we can take time, and always allow ourselves the choice to pull back and switch attention. By becoming aware of our capacities and limits, finding skilful ways to increase what resources us, we can use titration (a term from chemistry) to gradually add drops of what is painful into awareness, surrounding it with spaciousness. In this way we discover how to move from reaction to response and skilful regulation, regaining a window of tolerance, where we think more clearly, feel present and safe enough.

This is a training ground for sustaining compassion and needs care and time. In the process of discovering what helps and hinders regulation, we learn the signals that show it is too overwhelming to keep direct experience of body in awareness, and what else can help. If you are holding a process with yourself or others where anyone becomes dysregulated or starts to panic, it's important to call on resources and experienced people skilled in trauma work.

CREATIVE EXPLORATION

Taking in the space around you is one way to support emotional regulation.

Explore this in a structured way, looking right, left, up, down, forwards, and behind you. As you look in each direction take several conscious breaths, inhaling and exhaling.

What effect does this have on your system?

Repeat if needed.

To extend this, let your eyes trace the edges of walls, windows, doors, furniture as you look in each direction.

Images of self

While honouring the pain that may be housed in our physical systems, we can also employ the sense of spaciousness and possibility to explore a more malleable and playful relationship to our 'selves'. When the lens points only to the stories of loss and lack it can be limiting and shut down the doorways to greater freedom. The particular stories of our lives – the pains and pleasures, losses and gains – are essential, but they don't have to be the only thing that defines us. When we come into a caring relationship with our embodiment it can be a dance of dedication to how each moment arises and is encountered through the senses; at the same time there can be a broader lens, curious and open. From the thirteenth-century Zen master Dogen:

> To study the Way is to study the self. To study the self is to forget the self. To forget the self is to become intimate with, and awakened by, all things of the universe.[57]

This points to a radical mutuality, the thinning of borders between the illusions of self and other in the service of clear seeing and liberation.

As my conversation with Zohar and Nathan continues, we explore some of the nuances of self in relation to compassion:

> Nathan: In Dharma teachings there's a thrust towards the self being not as real as you think. For someone who cares this can feel like cutting a hole in the bucket. We need to be on fire, to have an image of 'someone who's going to come and do something really great'. But we can also have another image: 'I don't have anything to offer, my batteries are completely drained, my last efforts were futile.' We're necessarily signing up to feeling let down by ourselves, or by others for not joining us. There's a relationship with the winds of hope and despair. If our efforts are tied to hope and that hope is tied to incremental progress over time, what will we do when we're faced with ongoing racial injustice, gender inequality, homophobia, continuing climate destruction? Should we search for reasons to be hopeful in the dust? Or transcend that to a different creation of the self? One that is drawn simply towards, as Spike Lee said, 'doing the right thing'.

> Zohar: To see how the self gets built up within the realms of caring and service, and to see how we can untangle and unbind. Not because the self is bad but because getting tangled in it leads to suffering and diminishes our capacity.

> Nathan: As we move along, we realize that the not-self teachings can be transcended in the skilful fabrication of selves over time. We notice the ones that entrap and ensnare us, and we notice the ones that move us out of that. Then we're engaged in a deep dance with dependent origination.

Can I dare to linger in pausing, eyes closed, even as the laptop teeters on my knees, to raise the arms and ease the upper back? Hear the vertebrae ping and crackle as the hours voice themselves and ask for care, as the 'overdiligent self' recedes, allowing room for the one who remembers to stop, have a shimmy, sway like a tree in the wind, and respond to what is needed.

CREATIVE EXPLORATION

Experiment with engaging in the next task with the intention of restfulness in the midst of activity.

What do you notice? Can there be kindness towards any over-effort?

What image of yourself is forming as you pause or as you engage?

Body and bypassing

We have multilayered relationships with our bodies and are more – or less – aware of them at different times. The Irish writer James Joyce describes a character called Mr Duffy, who 'lived at a little distance from his body, regarding his own acts with doubtful side-glances'.[58]

Survival mechanisms and coping strategies can keep us, to some degree, at a distance from our bodies. Cultural and embodied identities also pile on the pressure towards disembodiment. Can we respect these histories and mechanisms, and learn how to invite awareness to gather, regather, even for a moment, with the felt bodily sense, here and now, resting on the support of the ground beneath us?

Becoming more embodied mitigates the pull to bypass lived experience through numbing, overwork, saviourism, and the spiritual bypassing that is a potential side-effect of contemplative practice. Bodies' processes move more slowly than thoughts, they remind us to pause, send strong signals when they are overwhelmed or ignored, and sometimes insist that we listen. In recent decades, our bodies have had to become static for long periods in front of screens, and our nervous systems have become umbilically connected to smartphones. These changes have a powerful impact on embodiment.

The motivation to care and act is embedded in lived experience. We may have learned to be vigilant to survive, there may have been an urgent need to get to safety as quickly and reliably as we could. In our adult lives there will be emergencies that need response. The pathways these crises imprint on the body can become reflexes and habit patterns that no longer serve us, manifesting as hypervigilance and a tendency to catastrophize.

Rest and kindness offer soothing to a nervous system that tends to fire quickly at any possible sources of alarm. To return to the body is to open a pathway for rest to take root, for resilience to grow and wise response to flourish. 'The body is a sacred book,' says Dharma teacher Leela Sarti, 'it is the teaching.'[59]

Restless night and pelting dreams
yet morning brings a question:
what if I was diligent caretaker
of this jangling body I call my own?

I move about and practise patience
as if I believed in it, as if doubt
was not always the sole trader here.[60]

CREATIVE EXPLORATION

 Guided Meditation – Pausing

With closed eyes or a softened gaze, lengthen the out-breath, allow the body's natural deflation to loosen your muscles, and let them relax towards the ground. Sigh as you exhale. Trace the downwards movement of skin, muscle, and bone. Track it all the way down to the sacrum and pelvic area, the sitting bones, the legs, to the soles of the feet. If you are lying down, tune in to the back of the body, all the places where it is in contact with the support beneath you.
Imagine the body is a lake full of sediment. When the lake is undisturbed, the sediment begins to settle, the water clarifies.

Moving for change

COP27 is taking place in Egypt. Around the globe demonstrations call on multinationals to stop extracting fossil fuels, and demand that world leaders act. I'm outside Norwich City Hall with my sister-in-law and young niece and nephew. The children are loudly impatient at having to stand about and listen to speeches they can't hear and don't understand. What are we doing, when can we have lunch? We are here partly to remember their dad, my brother, who took them to climate protests when they were in pushchairs, and who died one year ago.

Then the march forms, we pick up our cardboard banner with its blue- and green-crayoned planet Earth and start shuffling along the road. Simply putting one foot in front of the other shifts the energy, alleviates frustration. Though we cannot compete with shops drawing in the crowds for Christmas bargains, it is good to move together in the unseasonal autumn heat, in the company of strangers, walking and chanting through the cobbled streets.

Milla Gregor founded Movement for Change and offers wellbeing and resilience support for charities and change-makers, addressing burnout and overwhelm at systemic, organizational, and individual levels.[61] Her background is in the voluntary sector, non-violence, coaching, and yoga, and she is a long-term meditator. She sees movement practice as a useful way into embodiment, and thus into nourishment and flourishing, and considers that social justice is inextricably tied to this. 'Our ability to thrive', she says, 'is directly related to the quality of our relationships with ourselves, others, our communities, and with the natural and non-human world.' I met Milla on retreat and later crossed paths through the Mindfulness and Social Change Network; when we reconnect on Zoom she confirms what I've seen in my own experience and in working with others:

> Some people find it much easier to move rather than sit still as a means towards developing steady embodied awareness. In the charity sector there is so much burnout, there's trauma in one's own field, in the agencies and in the system, and it can seem as though you're working with incessant conflict and stress. The stress comes both from being exposed to systemic injustice and from the constant pressures on funding and capacity. People aren't really looking after

themselves. Often they are carrying so much tension that, if you ask them to sit still and connect with their experience, their attention just bounces off. A large amount of my work is around conflict – enabling people to become conflict-competent – and, without being able to connect with your physical experience, to know what you're feeling when you're dysregulated, you can't begin to relate to others, regain your window of tolerance, or recognize the needs that underlie strong emotions.[62]

Milla finds that movement can be a more accessible way into contemplative practice, either because it's less of a leap from daily-life activities for those with little experience of meditation, or because it can be presented with fewer connotations of mysticism and religion. Movement can begin very simply, for instance raising and lowering the arms, stepping, shaking – or even silly dancing. Sometimes people are holding on to so much that they need to start with strong movement such as yoga sequences. For many, the stillness at the end of a movement session, such as lying down for the last minutes of yoga, might be the only time they have permission simply to rest, to not be 'doing something'. This can be the most valuable part of the whole endeavour, in terms of personal resourcing, development, and even insight.

CREATIVE EXPLORATION

Take a moment to move, perhaps circling your hands or raising your arms or lifting your feet and legs. Repeat this a few times, co-ordinating with an in-breath and out-breath if that's comfortable. What do you notice?

What helps you come into greater contact with your embodied experience?

Did you forget to dance?

Refuge

The reception area of an immigration tribunal hearing centre. Rows of chairs bolted to the floor; in each corner anxious groups, mainly people of colour. I'm waiting to be summoned into the courtroom, while my friend is cross-questioned by a Home Office lawyer. Their claim for asylum on grounds of sexual orientation has been refused, and they are appealing against the decision. If unsuccessful, they may be deported to the country from which they've fled. I'm praying to anyone who will listen. Please keep them safe.

The questioning in these courtrooms is aimed at undermining the appellant and witnesses, punching holes in their credibility. There is a field of profound trauma: the appellant's trauma, the trauma of the LGBTQ community group who are here to support them, and the sustained trauma of homophobia and racism.

The body is not a refuge in this moment. A compassion chant comes to mind, and starts to circle in my head, bringing seconds of relief and distraction. Some calm opens and more possibilities appear. I sense the firm contact between my back and the seat, fixed as it is to the carpet and floor beneath. I stand up and walk around the room, taking in the shape of walls and windows.

Another friend arrives to stand as witness to the appellant's identity. She has survived this system and, though it continues to leave its mark, she is on the other side of it, working in health care and studying for a degree. We hug, leaning into each other, wordless. As well as the systemic hostility of the immigration system and the racialized trauma rooted in the history of this land, there are other factors. There is courage, love, resistance.

With greater calm, compassion expands. The bonds that have tightened around a fixed self, a 'someone who has to get it right', begin to loosen. The potential for true solidarity comes alive.

As we wait, I consider including the Home Office lawyer and the judge in the field of compassion. At first with the thought of aiming a blindingly intense beam of goodwill to influence their decision, but then with the realization that they too are human beings rather than enemies to be conquered. I consider the effect of sitting in windowless courtrooms for days on end, hearing testimonies of deep pain. When I'm called into the court, I try to look them in the eye and respond as carefully as I can.

Sound

For some people, and in some situations, mindfulness of body is not helpful or effective. This can be due to life conditions and circumstances, or the ways in which our embodied identities have been the targets of violence, marginalization, or threat.

In locations where I feel vulnerable as female-bodied or as a queer person, muscles flinch and contract; hypervigilance comes to the fore. Anxiety constricts freedom and narrows view. In the language of trauma awareness, the window of tolerance is diminished or lost. Exploring this response in a safe setting, I recall times of physical attack or verbal threat, and the survival strategies developed to protect myself. Some of these include a distancing from the moment-to-moment bodily sensations, or a default instinct of mistrust.

Using sound as an anchor is one way to support a caring response to embodied threat. Just like the range of felt sensations, sounds have a rich texture and spectrum – near and far, quiet and loud, pleasant and unpleasant. Sound attunes awareness to the space around and above us, which reduces the contraction of habitual responses. We can connect with the space around the sounds, the great silence from which they arise and to which they return. If tuning in to sound and spaciousness leads to spacing out and dissociating, we can direct awareness to the refuge of the solid ground beneath us, extending in all directions, both connected to us and vastly greater than us. We can also make sounds – humming, vocalizing, chanting – to reconnect with breath, embodiment, and ground. 'To listen to a leaf fall', writes Zenju Earthlyn Manuel, 'is an uninterrupted conversation with the earth. Listening is the lifeline to the deepest peace possible.'[63]

Avalokitesvara is the embodiment of compassion in Buddhist iconography. In Chinese the figure is female and known as Kwanyin – the listening, or listener, to the sounds of the world – in the Tibetan tradition becoming the male bodhisattva Chenrezig, the one who looks upon all beings with the eye of compassion.

Immensely popular and portrayed in many forms and variations throughout Buddhist countries, this beloved icon symbolizes the intrinsic connection between listening and compassion, and embodies the listening that is at the heart of contemplative practice. They are sometimes portrayed with one foot extended, stepping down from a meditation seat to respond to suffering. All-seeing and all-hearing, they are called on at times of personal and collective distress. One image shows them with a thousand arms, each offering a practical or symbolic antidote to pain. In another they recline regally, listening, and responding compassionately from a place of deep ease.

Dr Miriam Rose Ungunmerr Baumann, Aboriginal Artist, Educator, and Elder, reflects on the word, concept, and spiritual practice that is *dadirri* (da-did-ee) from the Ngan'gikurunggurr and Ngen'giwumirri languages of the Aboriginal peoples of the Daly River region (Northern Territory, Australia):

The identity we have with the land is sacred and unique. ... What I want to talk about is another special quality of my people. ... It is our most unique gift. ... In our language this quality is called dadirri. It is inner, deep listening and quiet, still awareness.

Dadirri recognises the deep spring that is inside us. We call on it and it calls to us. ... It is something like what you call 'contemplation'.

When I experience dadirri, I am made whole again. I can sit on the riverbank or walk through the trees; even if someone close to me has passed away, I can find my peace in this silent awareness. There is no need of words. ...

In our Aboriginal way, we learnt to listen from our earliest days. We could not live good and useful lives unless we listened. ... We learnt by watching and listening, waiting and then acting. Our people have passed on this way of listening for over 40,000 years... There is no need to reflect too much and to do a lot of thinking. It is just being aware.[64]

To respond congruently with care requires deep listening – listening inwardly and learning to listen to others with humility and patience. When opposing voices become difficult to hear, opinions polarize, and fracture lines are exacerbated through social media and manipulated by politicians. In the run-up to the 2020 US election, amid escalating tension, volunteers in rural and small-town Michigan went from door to door, engaging with older, white constituents on issues of racism and immigration.[65]

Deep Canvassing is not your traditional door-knocking campaign. It's not a campaign at all. These are longer conversations, and they require an ability to start where people are at without judgement. We ask people why they feel the way they do, and we share how we think about this subject and how that thinking came to be. We don't try to persuade people. These sorts of intimate conversations require letting go of the politics of divide and conquer, and the idea that isolating ourselves keeps us safer. This didn't always go well... but on the best days the conversations were transformative. Not just for the people on whose door we knocked, but for ourselves.[66]

What can be heard when we offer radical empathy to ourselves and to others? We may become more sensitive to what is usually ignored, or notice tendencies to make assumptions and rush to conclusions.

One summer afternoon I lead a group of singers in an outdoor writing workshop in the Scottish hills of Dumfries and Galloway. We walk slowly into a forest, then sit down amongst the trees and just listen. Though we initially feel awkward and self-conscious, soon the listening deepens. Sounds are amplified. We blend into the woodscape. Some folks out hiking pass close by without seeing us. We overhear a fragment of their conversation: 'You could lose yourself here.' The song we write begins, 'In the silence where nothing's ever quiet...' and includes elements from the natural world, different languages, long notes from a cello, body percussion.

Slowing down and resting deepens a capacity for listening and becomes the foundation for creative responses.

CREATIVE EXPLORATION

What can you hear in this moment? Nearby and far away?

What enables you to listen more deeply?

Can you listen from the back of the body? From the shoulder blades? From the heels?

Can you tune in to the space between sounds? The space between everything?

On stopping

At dawn we climb onto the roof of the Gloria Hotel in Jerusalem's Old City. The view is serene. Setting down borrowed cushions we sit in meditation. I glance at my companions: an Australian who has made a pilgrimage to Mount Kailash, Tibet, an American who is a nun in Cambodia, and my friend Sheena from Sheffield.

From here the city seems peaceful: skyline of ancient and modern, TV aerials, satellite dishes, washing lines, traffic noise from the Jaffa Gate. Walking Jerusalem's streets I'm overwhelmed by history, by stories carried in the marble steps and walls. The smooth dimples and curves worn by centuries of feet and carts. I close my eyes and sense the hard surface beneath, the rhythm of breathing, smells of petrol, dust, and bread baking.

Thoughts arise of the day ahead, the journey to East Jerusalem where we will sit in the shade of a huge awning and listen to speeches. Then a silent vigil in the tradition of the international peace group Women in Black who have organized this conference. We will bear witness at Qalandia Gate, the main checkpoint from the West Bank where queues of Palestinians wait for hours to be let through – for work, for school, for university, for hospital appointments, for birth, for death. Alongside, the separation wall that snakes back and forth, imprisoning, dividing.

> Between September 2000 and October 2004
> at Israeli army checkpoints
> sixty-one women delivered babies,
> thirty-six of them stillborn.

> Below the skin of the numbers
> stretch yourself into memory or imagination
> and see yourself blockaded, labouring,
> able neither to go back nor forward.

> A subtler poet would work in a biblical allusion
> tie a knot with Herod,
> with the deadly twins
> of history and religion.

> I only want forceps to midwife sense,
> a scalpel to dissect, lay wide the fear
> that keeps an eighteen-year-old's rifle
> aiming steadily into the ambulance.[67]

A bell rings. End of meditation. We open our eyes, breathe out a collective sigh. The city sounds are swelling as the day gathers pace. Here on the roof there's space for a while to rest and feel the hard comfort of concrete underneath us. We pick up our cushions and slowly descend the stairs.

Fast forward twelve years. The minibus draws up at a disused house in the West Bank village where a dozen of us will live for ten days to assist with the olive harvest. Walking into the groves as the sun sets, we find our feet on the rock-strewn earth and pause. Gnarled trees with grey-green leaves stand with us. We each choose a tree and lean into it. I find one whose limbs cradle me.

Rubbing dust off the purple-green fruit, the oil gleams. I'm captivated.

'It's all about the trees!', I murmur as we return.

A white-and-orange kitten stares at us from her perch on a mountain of rubble and rubbish. The call to prayer echoes across the valley. A woman trudges uphill with a donkey laden with sacks of olives. Our hosts have come to welcome us with dates and tea, and of course olive oil. I see the trees in all of them.

Though only an hour's drive from Tel Aviv, we've crossed many borders: physical, psychological, political. We stopped en route to take in the Wall and its watchtowers, longer and taller than in 2005, encircling Palestinian villages, cutting people off from their groves, houses, and land.

After some days in the olive groves, we stop for silence and contemplation – time to meet and listen to all sides of the conflict: Israeli settlers, peace activists, Israeli and Palestinian former soldiers and combatants. We have the honour of visiting Issa Souf, a meditation practitioner and peace activist of many decades, shot and disabled by Israeli soldiers in 2001. We learn of his vision for the Garden of Hope Mindfulness Centre in the West Bank.[68]

After adapting to the rhythms of harvest and connecting with the families who generously host us, it is challenging to put the brakes on. I want the momentum to continue, longing for the trees' companionship, the fruits' smooth shininess as fingers comb through leaves, olives softly pelting tarps laid over the stony ground. Slowing down is an interruption and a source of guilt. While we meditate, families in the olive groves are under intense pressure. Trees left unharvested risk being cut down, the land confiscated by the Israeli army or settlers. But stopping gives time to absorb and digest the bigger picture. To educate ourselves about the conflict, take in the impact of multigenerational trauma, the harassment and land grabs, the constant threat. Pausing means we re-engage with renewed energy and respect, returning to the trees with more patience and care.

Zohar reflects on the path of practice and service in deepening compassion and wisdom:

> People often ask me: 'How can you keep going back to Palestine when nothing changes, it just gets worse?' Yes, there is that clarity, but that's not the measure. I go back because it's the right thing to do, and not only because it's the right thing to do, it's the *best* thing to do. I used to have an image of the heart getting broken again and again. The heart breaking is part of loosening the sense of self and of separation. A cultivation of this tender equanimity that understands I matter but it's not just down to me. And there is also joy! We're talking about rest, but joy is important, to let ourselves be touched and nourished by what we do.

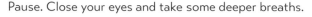

CREATIVE EXPLORATION

Pause. Close your eyes and take some deeper breaths.

Imagine a parcel arrives with a message:

> This is a gift of absolute permission to put tasks aside,
> leave things unfinished, imperfect, and incomplete.
> Let the busy neurons in your cells slowly settle.
> Atoms in your bone marrow, arteries' tingling electrons –
> all can sigh deeply and hang up their hats.

Dial down the volume on the infinite demands for your time and attention.

Find a comfortable chair, put your feet up, or lie down.

Let your body move if it wants, held by silence or by music.

If neither resting nor moving fits the bill, listen deeply, indoors, outdoors, or through an open door or window.

Absorb ease. Resting may reveal buried feelings – let it be a wide-brimmed container.

Chapter 2
BEFRIENDING

*A kindly hospitable person is like a great banyan tree
growing on the side of roads that welcomes weary travellers
with its cool shade and soothes their tiredness.*

The Jataka Tales[69]

An orientation for life

I met Jaya Rudgard when she taught a retreat for my local meditation group. Though slightly in awe of her years as a Buddhist monastic, I offered to host her. She was an easy companion, and anxiety soon evaporated. Since then, I've come to deeply appreciate her kindness and wisdom as a teacher and colleague.

On that first retreat I was struck by the way Jaya sat calmly back in a chair as she guided the group, legs folded beneath her. Apparently relaxed, friendly, at ease. Sharp contrast to my mind fizzing with organizer-thoughts: 'Is everyone OK? Should I do this? What about that?'

Jaya describes the influences that led her towards the Dharma:

I'm half Chinese and as a child I had great-grandmothers in Hong Kong who were devout Buddhists and went on retreat with the nuns. Although I was raised as Anglican, my mum said that the best Christians she knew were the Buddhists, so I was primed to look in that direction. I got into reading about Buddhism in my teens, and at seventeen, by a stroke of luck, I took myself to stay at Chithurst, a monastery in West Sussex. It was a pivotal experience. At that point I was on a trajectory towards more conventional educational things, but in my late twenties I decided to become a nun in that community.

In those teenage years Jaya had a significant encounter:

There weren't many Dharma books available, but I picked up what I could find in my local bookshop and came across a translation of the *Metta Sutta*.[70] I copied it into my notebook of precious quotes where it had pride of place. I found the sutta inspiring as an orientation for life. As well as metta, it talks about being able, upright, humble and not conceited, gentle in one's speech and so on. The central passage about metta for all living beings, the weak and strong, the big and small, was such a wonderful kind of cosmic aspiration. It was more relatable and seemed to be a happy fusion of an ancient Greek philosopher and a good Christian (both of which I aspired to be).

The sutta that Jaya refers to can be found in Resource 1, on p.173. 'Metta' comes from the Pali word *mitta* meaning 'friend', and can be translated as 'friendliness', 'befriending', 'loving-kindness', 'goodwill', or 'benevolence'; I will use these terms interchangeably.[71] Friendliness is the ground that protects and nourishes the development of compassion. Without genuine warmth and active goodwill, the aspiration to care degenerates into pity.

Friendliness sounds appealing. Who doesn't want to be welcomed as the cooling shade of a tree welcomes foot-sore, thirsty travellers? Who doesn't want genuine friends who show up when needed and put aside other concerns to listen and respond? But friendship can be fraught. Whether in the playground or classroom, in a work setting or family gathering, we know what it's like to be ignored or rejected. We care about what other people think of us; it matters whether we are more – or less – likeable or popular than others. Offering friendship and kindness to others can also feel challenging. We may wonder whether it means we should like or love or approve of everyone. Whether we will be taken for granted or misused. This is the territory we encounter when we explore the cultivation of goodwill, gradually expanding our capacity, becoming more and more willing to turn towards all aspects of others and ourselves, including the barriers and doubts, with an intention of friendliness.

Opening the door
    mid-grudge
and the touch of
    cool air
reminds me
    of the intention
    for befriending –
this too
    the sullen step
    the grating thought.[72]

CREATIVE EXPLORATION

Take a few slower breaths.

Bring to mind a person who supports or inspires you, a loving friend or relative, a teacher, a role model. Imagine and sense their presence, recalling something helpful they have done or said, or simply their way of being.

Tune in to any thoughts, feelings, or bodily sensations that feel warm and appreciative towards them, and notice the effect of this on you.

Gift of gravity

In the grainy, monochrome images of Neil Armstrong and Buzz Aldrin walking on the moon in 1969, their steps are alternately clunky and graceful. Videos of the International Space Station show cables slowly writhing as if animate. The astronauts' lives rely on them being attached. Every handhold, foothold, or restraint is vital and can prevent injury or death.

Our bodies have evolved alongside the force of gravity, and are unable to stay in zero- or microgravity for long without becoming unwell. Weightlessness has negative effects on human health; our physiological systems begin to change and atrophy. Likewise, an embodied connection to the surfaces beneath us, and the ability to remember and tune in to those surfaces, is somatically and psychologically restorative. Gravity is a gift we often take for granted.

In the *Satipatthana Sutta* mindfulness of the body begins with finding a suitable place to practise:

> And how does a practitioner dwell observing an aspect of the body?
> It's when a practitioner – gone to a wilderness, or to the root of a tree, or to an empty hut – sits down cross-legged, with their body straight, and focuses their mindfulness right there. Just mindful, they breathe in. Mindful, they breathe out.[73]

Mourning the death of a soldier killed in the First World War, Wilfred Owen wrote: 'Was it for this the clay grew tall?'[74] When the clay of our body rests fully on the clay of the earth, we tap into something greater than ourselves, a vastness that offers solace. It opens the door to compassionate self-regulation and a capacity to dilute difficulty so its impact is less concentrated.

Environmental activist Julia Butterfly Hill lived for 738 days at the top of a giant redwood to prevent it being cut down and to preserve the surrounding forest. She describes her first ascent into the tree:

> A rope that's about the width of my thumb comes snaking down from so far above I can't see where it begins. I went for it, but the perilous condition of my life on a teeny-tiny rope with a harness held together by duct tape started sinking in. ... I felt this calling, telling

me to just close my eyes and put my hands and my feet up against the tree, and when I did, I found all this energy flowing through me back down into the roots. It immediately grounded me. I just kept my eyes on the tree, and I made it to the top, 180 feet up, in about fifteen minutes.[75]

Jaya describes how this connection with ground intersects with developing metta:

I make a lot of feeling and sensing the relationship with Earth. When I'm annoyed or feeling let down, I recall that the Earth has always been there, and always will be, my life is not possible without her. Gratitude is a good catalyst for metta, and I feel gratitude for life through acknowledging my embodied relationship with the Earth and my surroundings. As a kinaesthetic person, I was always into yoga. Now I practise qi gong, which emphasizes our energetic connection with earth, through the imagery of trees and their constant symbiotic exchange with the Earth. I think metta is the generative energy of life.

CREATIVE EXPLORATION

Sense or look downwards to the surfaces below your body. Allow the shapes, colours, forms to register in awareness.

Explore the textures, temperature, material of these surfaces with your fingers, hands, and feet. Wiggle your toes on the ground, enjoy the feel of cloth or wood, cushion, carpet, grass, or earth.

Using sight, touch, movement, or imagination, recall the earth that is underneath you, and bring to mind some of the ways it makes your life possible.

Kindness? Really?

When kindness is unfamiliar, we can create maps, testing out and finding the best routes towards it. Kindness may not be the right word; it can have overtones that are exclusive or oppressive, or be used to cover up and pretend. Lama Rod Owens writes:

> Sometimes I do struggle with the word 'kindness'. Frankly, it reminds me of all the white people in my life who have been kind to me but have hurt me when that kindness gives way to these old historical and habitual allegiances to whiteness and its dominance over my body and mind.[76]

The near enemy that masquerades as metta is said – by Buddhaghosa, the fifth-century-CE author of an influential commentary on early Buddhist discourses – to be selfish, greedy affection. In a twenty-first-century context this could include the shallow, conditional 'kindness' described by Lama Rod, or a pretended niceness, the impulse to stick a heart on a social media post because a hundred others have, or because it will look good.

We may not have been conditioned to practise authentic kindness, to express it and recognize it in ourselves or in others.

When Jaya and I speak about disentangling metta from attachment or attraction, she points to the pitfalls of translating 'metta' as 'loving-kindness':

> It's easy to feel friendliness towards people that we like or are attracted to, which is why the English word 'love' can be confusing. The intention of metta is unconditional friendliness, not dependent on whether we like somebody, or they like us back, or we get something out of it. It's 'I wish you well just as you are', not 'I wish you well so that you can change and be the kind of person I want you to be so that I can be happy.' Which is very different from the way a lot of us approach trying to have a loving relationship with people! Kindness also sometimes introduces a sense of I *should* be kind, and 'should' is not a helpful word.

When I was introduced to the practice of cultivating loving-kindness (*metta-bhavana* or 'bringing metta into being') I was mystified. The teacher suggested we use phrases to wish ourselves well, such as 'May I be healthy and well.' Seeing my bewilderment, they encouraged me to imagine a sensation of warmth in my chest. I looked down at my torso; I tried to picture a warm glow, like the orange aura used to advertise a brand of breakfast cereal. Nothing.

Buddhaghosa is adamant that

first of all [metta] should be developed only towards oneself, doing it repeatedly thus: 'May I be happy and free from suffering' or 'May I keep myself free from enmity, affliction and anxiety and live happily.'[77]

He is at pains to allay concerns that this could conflict with teachings on selflessness, quoting this passage:

I visited all quarters with my mind
Nor found I any dearer than myself;
Self is likewise to every other dear;
Who loves themself will never harm another.[78]

Though this sounds logical, for years I viewed metta as a good idea but impossible to practise towards myself. I worked diligently on extending it towards others – the ones who inspired me, the ones I liked, the irritating and annoying, and those I didn't know – but I was doubtful about its effects. The practice was comforting to some extent, and I could see that goodwill was more useful than grumbling, but it was mainly an intellectual process.

The traditional metta phrases can be helpful anchors to realign and centre attention, but can divert us from developing an embodied sense of these qualities. Words hold power, but they have limitations and are not always the most accessible channel. Other doorways include images, bodily sensations, movement, sights, sounds, textures that can guide us into developing warmth and authentic well-wishing. It takes time, experimentation, and patience to connect with the brahma-viharas in ways that are meaningful for our direct experience.

While investigating metta, an image came of freely given kindness:

Mercy has a thousand arms that curve
from right and left towards the sternum
like graceful, patient waiters
offering platters of comfort.[79]

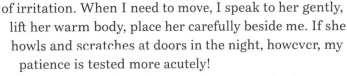

One starting place is the warmth
we can feel towards animals,
such as those in our care, the
dogs, cats, chickens, rabbits,
hamsters that we call pets. As I write
this, Tabitha, our elderly tabby cat,
eases herself into the space between
the keyboard and my stomach, purrs,
curls up, and falls asleep. Almost
unconsciously, I make space for her,
adjust my hands, set aside a moment

of irritation. When I need to move, I speak to her gently,
lift her warm body, place her carefully beside me. If she
howls and scratches at doors in the night, however, my
patience is tested more acutely!

The warmth we humans show our animal
companions is legendary – we easily see the
lovableness in them; it is also true that our species is
capable of limitless cruelty towards other animals. Some non-human
beings can be challenging objects of goodwill and kindness, and Jaya
describes her relationship with insects through a metta lens:

One of the first Dharma talks I heard was Ajahn
Sumedho on the need to have friendliness
even to insects, and to respect
them as sentient beings. Later
that summer I was on a family
holiday with lots of mosquitoes
and horseflies, and for the first time
made a practice of restraining my impulse
to swat them. At that point I could do it with

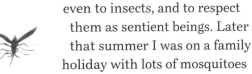

a degree of equanimity, and taste how different it felt to inhabit that attitude to life. I felt happier as a result, it led to more contentment, and in that space I noticed other people's irritability. It's like the benchmark changed for what was normal.

Can we extend this friendliness, or at least restraint of impulses to annihilate, to ourselves, however we are, with our habits, flaws, and foibles? Traditional ways of practising the brahma-viharas originate in the *Metta Sutta*, the same one that Jaya copied into her notebook as a teenager. The image here is of a loving parent, willing to risk everything, including their own life, to protect their child. It can be hard to relate to this if your parents have not protected you. But we can tune into the care and warmth offered, if not by other humans, then from the animal and more-than-human world, nature, landscapes that have nourished and wanted nothing in return. This quality of protectiveness establishes and builds a ground of friendliness.

CREATIVE EXPLORATION

What words for metta work best for you?

What images are most helpful?

How, in this moment, can you tune in to the softness of the body? Perhaps the gentle touch of clothes on your skin, an image of the body melting into the surface beneath?

Blocks

Kindness to oneself is the foundation of sustaining, resilient compassion. Unless the vessel is replenished, it will run dry. And no replenishment will happen if the container is stoppered with a big sign: 'No Refills Allowed. Not Worthy.'

There are infinite justifications for unworthiness. Some are rooted in guilt, fear, numbness, others in systemic negation through race, culture, gender, class, sexuality, and other identities.

We can take small steps. Micro-moments of breathing in and out, allowing the body to find the ground, soften and loosen. Split seconds of acting as if we too, with no strings attached, deserve friendship, positive regard. Resisting the voices – internal and external – that deny care and love. Unconditional metta includes befriending its opposing mind-states, including unfriendliness, irritation, and anger.

Jaya recalls how she uncovered habit patterns of self-judgement:

In my first few weeks of living in the monastery, I did something – totally innocently – that hurt another person. When I was beating myself up for my mistake, one of the nuns said, 'Would you talk to *me* in that way?' I was twenty-nine and it was the first time I clocked how my way of relating to myself was profoundly unkind. I'd come from an achievement-driven world where it's normal to use ridicule and bullying to get people to do what you want, and that was how I'd learned to relate to myself. It was a shift to realize, just as in that sutta I'd transcribed fifteen years earlier, that metta is for all living beings, which includes oneself. We often hold ourselves to higher standards than we hold other people, which is why we can be so hard on ourselves.

Like all practice, this is non-linear. There can be moments of touching deeply into a source of tenderness; and other moments of letting go to reveal another layer of blame. The exploration demands great patience. Can you approach and offer metta to this one wherever and however you are right now, with unique form and complexity? Giving kindliness and respect with no strings attached, as if you were a good friend, the beloved animal, or the plant stretching towards the sun, a bird soaring in the sky.

here too
kindness for the
nervous, sweating
anticipating

here too
pausing
let tenderness come

and the gunboats
of perfectionism
recede
into the dark[80]

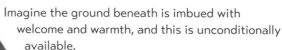

CREATIVE EXPLORATION

 Guided Meditation – Befriending

Imagine the ground beneath is imbued with welcome and warmth, and this is unconditionally available.

Breathe in from this warm and friendly ground and let this breath fill your body.

If the ground feels inaccessible, tune in to the space around you, and, as the life-giving oxygenated air enters your lungs, connect with its support and benevolence.

Field of intentionality

When befriending is a struggle, it is helpful to pull back and consider motivation and intention. Motivation energizes us to respond to our heart's calling. Intention, in a Dharma context, is threefold: renunciation or simplification, goodwill, and non-violence. These three strands clarify motivation by putting harmlessness, and its positive correlate compassion, front and centre. Intention asks how our response, including thoughts and words as well as action, can reduce suffering, lead away from harm to ourselves and others, and towards greater ease and wellbeing. Motivation and intention have many layers, often revealed by stopping and stepping back. When we stop in the midst of habitual patterns, or realize that we're on automatic pilot, there is the possibility for greater awareness of embodied thoughts, feelings, and mind-states, and the impulses behind actions get clearer. Do they head away from harm and violence, and towards harmlessness, compassion, and letting go?

Most circumstances involve balancing motivation and intention with response-ability, sensitivity, possibility, capability. Snow is falling, the temperature is below zero, I trudge up to the chicken coop to close our seven hens in for the night. They're huddled together on the perch. Recently re-homed from commercial egg farms where they've lived indoors in artificial light and heat, they haven't yet grown full sets of feathers. I consider bringing them into the house, then remember the potential mess, the cat's reaction, the sleepless night. 'If you really cared...' a voice in my head begins. Someone else, in another set of conditions, would respond differently. My partner has been known to take them hot-water bottles. But right now, I try to consider all the factors and do the best I can for the welfare of all the beings involved, remembering that previous hens have survived colder conditions with fewer feathers, and that I can take them some warm feed in the morning.

Establishing intention is not a one-off act, it is a constant learning process. As part of this, greater sensitivity can be cultivated towards potentially harmful impacts of words, silences, actions, inactions, however well-intentioned, and we can learn to apologize and make amends when we cause harm. Larry Yang describes the establishment of East Bay Meditation Center (EBMC) in Oakland, California, with 'the vision of serving diverse communities that had not been on the radar or recognized by mainstream meditation centers'.[81] Included in the Agreements for Multicultural Interactions developed by EBMC is the importance of understanding the difference between intent and impact, acknowledging that focusing on intention, particularly when done by white people or other groups with social privilege, can be used to deny responsibility for causing harm.[82]

Jaya links the foundation of intention with the direction of befriending. As we make metta our direction, then metta reveals itself to be more than something generated by a narrow sense of self:

> Metta brings connectivity, a field of intentionality that one can inhabit. Rather than something you pump out from the inside, you tune yourself to a wavelength, plug into an interpersonal energy field. Just in holding the intention of metta, having this conversation, and thinking about people who might read this, there's a meeting place where we're plugging into the same field.

Imagining a greater field of intention gives support for the many moments when metta is not accompanied by warm or pleasant feelings. Sometimes even the distant prospect of friendliness has us running in the opposite direction. The brahma-viharas are not emotions (in the sense of happiness etc. in response to external circumstances) or feeling-tones (pleasant, unpleasant, or neutral), though they can be accompanied by these. It may not feel agreeable or pleasant to practise metta, and yet, when we turn towards that intention, even where it seems counterintuitive, such as towards ourselves or towards a person we dislike, we expand our perception and learn how best to lessen reactivity. Even a moment of metta sets in motion the greater likelihood of a better future. Washing the dishes, I pause mid-grumble. The warm, soapy water reminds my hands of metta, and this filters into awareness, making harmony more likely in subsequent conversations about household chores. In the process I notice and gradually learn about the contrasting impacts of grudge or goodwill on my system.

Flowers of hope, fuel of despair

Lying on my back in the city centre, I sense the quiet breathing bodies around me, a samba band and their silent instruments, a hush where moments ago there were speeches and chants. It's one year since Sheffield City Council declared a climate emergency. We are responding to the lack of subsequent action with a die-in; later we will enter the town hall to question city councillors. I look up: blue sky, a smattering of cloud. The pavement is cold and hard, I wonder what's been trodden into it. Glad of my coat, I think of those living outdoors on winter streets.

A child's voice: 'I don't want to lie down! I want to run away!'

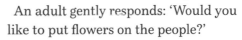

An adult gently responds: 'Would you like to put flowers on the people?'

A small hand places a paper rose on my chest.

I remember that I've laid down on this patch of pavement before, at silent vigils opposing the invasions of Afghanistan and Iraq.

March 2003. Brim-full with rage and grief, I've marched, written letters, sung, organized meetings, joined a peace symbol made of naked bodies, stood in candlelit parks. Teetering on the edge of burnout I join a bicycle blockade. In the morning rush hour we bring the city to a standstill. We have no plan, no words of explanation.

'I have to get my kids to school!' a driver yells.

'And the bombs are falling on Baghdad!' I yell back.

I feel justified and self-righteous. My response seems entirely appropriate; to spread the suffering might somehow diminish it.

In due course I recognize the despair that fuelled this response and am anguished at my lack of care for those caught in the gridlock. My motivation was revenge. I wanted to make someone suffer in a vain attempt to blot out my pain. Under this despair, concern for victims of war was mixed with the overwhelm of injustice, the terror of powerlessness. If you'd questioned whether my intentions were truly non-violent, I would have been insulted, but with hindsight the degree

65

of violence directed towards others and myself has become clearer.

Motivation is often complex; it connects to multiple strands of collective and personal histories, and the unravelling takes time. An intention of non-harm shines a light into motivation's corners, revealing hidden agendas, self-interest, strategies aimed at getting approval. It uncovers where the saviour, rescuer, and hero fantasies play out, the ways in which we might deny vulnerabilities by throwing ourselves into helping others.

Take a conscious breath. How is this landing? Can the untangling be done with self-compassion, with an intention of non-harm for oneself? Can the seeds of violence in our hearts and minds be investigated and understood, without subjecting them to the violence of repression? Following the compass direction that invites, indeed demands, congruence: 'There is no way to peace – peace is the way.'[83]

Going off course has dangers, and there are pitfalls when motivations aren't clear or intentions become blurred, often by the clamouring of the anxious self: am I good enough? What will others think of me? Is this the right way?

The Zen poet Ryokan says it well:

> If you point your cart north
> When you want to go south,
> How will you arrive?[84]

Can we set a course, knowing that patience and forgiveness are required for each step on the path, and that getting lost is inevitable? Remembering and forgetting: forgetting and remembering. The territory of forgetfulness and doubt is the ground of contemplative practice, its gifts are humility and a realignment with our humanity. When we remember and regain a path, it's a relief; the path comes into clearer focus, we resharpen our intention.

> Forgiveness – as the short day darkens –
> always more required than one imagined,
> and perhaps, after all,
> nothing to forgive,
> only a humanness,
> an appetite.[85]

CREATIVE EXPLORATION

Pause and find the ground. Tune in to your breath, the space around you, and whatever brings you more fully into the present.

Respond to these enquiries. If worry, self-consciousness, or performance pressure arise, acknowledge them and gently (or firmly) put them aside. You don't have to make sense or give definitive answers.

What moves you? What matters most to you?

How might you align your life with this?

Who and what will support you?

Dancing with Mara

In the creative process and the journey towards metta, as in any endeavour, doubt's voice can be a close companion. Working with people who want to write poems, novels, songs, or simply make a mark on the page, much of the support required is in identifying internalized messages of stultifying judgement. The critic tells young writers: 'You've had no experience of life, what can you possibly have to say?' It condemns older writers with: 'You've left it too late, time is running out, there's no point.' Replace 'writers' with 'human beings'. A creative path to sustaining compassion often loops back to seeing these inner questionings clearly, reconciling with them, recycling what is useful, and moving forward.

These messages have power because they are so close to us, they are intimate, speaking in our own voice, whispering to us when we are most vulnerable. They appear disguised as friends, as consolation.

A bus journey across the city. A man climbs on board and stays for a few stops, standing in the aisle, murmuring, then shouting to himself. His voice is that of an insatiably cruel critic. It holds his brief travel companions in its remorseless, overpowering sway; the tone is vicious yet recognizable. You're no good, you are in the way, you shouldn't be here, you're useless. To hear it loud and clear, with no possible exit, is shocking.

The inner critic, merchant of shame, has no shame itself and will attach to anything. It can stop us in our tracks, rendering us unable to speak or act. It can cause mental torment. It lies behind states of depression and anxiety. It assumes the voice and demeanour of the oppressor. In 'Eye to eye: Black women, hatred and anger' Audre Lorde writes of 'the iceberg' of hatred, 'that societal deathwish directed against us from the moment we were born Black and female'. She continues:

> Nothing I accept about myself can be used against me to diminish me. ... It is easier to deal with the external manifestations of racism and sexism than it is to deal with the results of those distortions internalized within our consciousness of ourselves and one another.[86]

The internalized judge readily adopts the voice of white supremacy and patriarchy; if we're queer, the voice of hetero-, cis-, and binary-normativity; it tells disabled people or those from working-class backgrounds to keep their heads well below the parapet, and not to draw attention. There are no toeholds, no crevices too small for it. Any chink can be exploited and used to wound.

The critic is an illusion, but it draws strength from the social bases of oppression, and from survival strategies and protective reflexes that proved their worth in the past but have outlived their use and become fossilized. Fed by familial, educational, and social structures that grade, compare, and anoint with failure or success, it can occupy a predominant place in our lives. A Buddhist understanding of the critic as empty, and thus without inherent permanent substance, can seem a pitiable response when the critic is in full swing. Yet, with metta as a foundation, this understanding can open a gap between a judgemental thought pattern and automatic compliance; in this gap there can be recognition and the realization that yielding is not compulsory. As the critic starts to take form, we learn to recognize its stirrings and become more attuned to its signals.

Mara, a central figure in the stories of early Buddhism, is – from a psychological perspective – the personification of criticism and doubt.

The word 'Mara' comes from a Sanskrit root and can be translated as 'causing death' or 'killing'. Mara appears to Gotama on the night of liberation, with their armies. They continue to appear throughout the Buddha's life, dancing attendance, baiting, undermining. Mara comes to laypeople and monastics alike, knowing exactly where the faultlines are, and which buttons to press. The bhikkhuni Soma, immersed in meditation at the foot of a tree, receives a visit from Mara in the form of internalized patriarchy:

> You're reaching beyond your capacity,
> that state is only for wise men,
> it's not possible for a woman
> with her measly amount of wisdom.[87]

The antidote in these encounters is that, the instant Mara is seen and known, the internal voices and impulses are recognized for what they are. As soon as the words 'I see you!' are spoken, Mara slinks off dejected and disappears. The spell is broken. In Soma's case she retorts by rebuffing Mara's focus on identity.

This moment of recognition seems simple but it's not easy, and the swift dismissal has a dramatic punch, but the timescale of response is probably longer. Recognition requires the development of mindful loving awareness, and, as we deepen in awareness, the onion layers of shame and self-criticism are revealed. This is not comfortable. In the process, we may become more sensitized to the violence within ourselves, and the violence in the world. Mindfulness of body is vital; the Buddha gives a range of similes for its importance. If Mara tries to demoralize those who have developed mindfulness of body, it will be like filling an already full jar, or trying to bounce a ball of string through a hardwood door, or lighting a fire with wet wood.[88]

As I surf the internet, algorithms draw me to things that appeal and shore up my sense of being right. I scroll to the comments on an article I agree with. There's a compulsion to read these and get hooked by the most disagreeable ones, forgetting there are trolls and bots in this cyber wilderness, posts manipulated by the agents of authoritarian states. The body contracts and shrinks. Breath becomes shallow. These quarrelsome voices continue to reverberate. I complain about them to anyone who listens, and inwardly debate with them. They have twinned with Mara; they throw me off balance. Doubt quick-steps and outpaces static versions of my better intentions, it tries to overpower any clear-eyed seeing that knows how best to care. It gives hopelessness the upper hand.

When we've developed an intention, set a course for sustaining compassion, we can depend on Mara turning up to the party with their wardrobe of costumes and disguises. They take many forms, including cynicism, despair, apathy, fear, and the compassion thought-police. Traditionally, Mara's armies include greed, hatred, delusion, boredom, hunger, thirst, craving, sloth and torpor, terror, uncertainty, malice, hypocrisy, stubbornness, gain, honour, renown, notoriety, and denigrating others.[89] Their forms have both a universal flavour and a particular resonance with our own conditions.

One of the critic's super-powers is to be able to change form when it is spotted. When we recognize a tendency to be judgemental of others or oneself, this recognition itself can provoke shame or despair, and an impulse of denial or self-punishment. The Buddha compares this reactivity to someone wounded by an arrow who immediately strikes themself with a second arrow. In the critic's context this manifests as the tendency, impelled by shame or guilt, to add another dose of distress to an already painful experience.[90]

If we tangle with the critic with the intention of abolishing it, we find ourselves locked in battle. Though sometimes it's necessary to stare the inner critic down, and firmly steer the mind towards another course, other more creative strategies are possible. Given that a combative approach often backfires, getting curious about and moving towards one's inner demons is a route favoured by both traditional teachings and contemporary psychology. Mara too can be encountered and addressed with an intention of metta. Hounded by tormenting monsters whose onslaught only intensified with his fear, Tibetan yogi Milarepa changed tack by putting his head right into their mouths. Only then did they transform, and pledge to protect him. Recognizing, inviting, and feeding your demons can turn them into allies.[91]

How can this prodigious energy be recycled into something creative?[92] Can we use it to hone our compassion for the ways in which it wreaks havoc in the world? Mara fuels corruption and tyranny, and Mara's power over us can also become tyrannical.

CREATIVE EXPLORATION

Before exploring the critic, check that you have enough emotional resilience, and friendliness towards yourself.

Write, draw, or express in any medium, from the point of view and in the voice of the inner critic, no holds barred, for three minutes. What do they really want? Allow the full response, including any humour.

Now explore from the point of view of a skilled mediator who can see all sides of the dynamic and knows that there is a way forward. We tend to see only dualistic options: 'with Mara' or 'without Mara', 'with shame' or 'without shame'. How can the ever-adaptable energy of the critic be recycled and creatively engaged as a helpful force? Write, draw, dance, or express in any medium the shape this could take.

Moving metta

Writing and editing the paragraphs above, I become aware that I've not moved in more than an hour. The light is fading. I close the laptop and put on my coat. It's stopped raining but everything's damp. Walking in and out of puddles I notice rocks swathed in emerald moss, rusted bracken, sludgy verges, soggy scraps of litter. Words ping around the mind, what to write next, what to change, what to add. But there is space here, and the familiar crunch of wellies on gravel. A friend walks towards me, emerging out of the twilight. We exchange good wishes and share our enjoyment at getting out of the house, defying the short, gloomy days.

Friendliness is a moveable feast. Even when disability or illness limit movement, metta can offer a necessary movement of the mind from habitual grooves.

For Jaya, movement has always been a refuge:

In some ways my first experiences of meditation were doing ballet classes as a little girl. Moving gently with soothing music puts the heart and mind in an open, soft, and tender space that is like the felt sense of metta. You can dance metta, you can probably play metta as a musician. You can cook metta as a chef, you can express metta through tending your garden or cooking for people or holding somebody's hand or singing and chanting.

Even the smallest of movements, a smile, a hand on the heart, can powerfully convey loving-kindness. A homeopathic dose of care. When I first encountered the practice of breathing and smiling from the Plum Village tradition, cynicism put up strong resistance. Through following Jaya's qi gong teaching, I've learned to invite a smile in the body as well as the face, as part of bringing together movement, breath, and inner attitude. Jaya reflects on how this can be a powerful aid for altering a downcast outlook:

The practice of the inner smile is a helpful metta practice. I don't have to have something to smile about, if I can just relax my body into a gesture of a smile it shifts the state of mind. A lot of people are initially sceptical, like it's not right to fake something, but shifting that embodied attitude has a profound effect on the mind. When you walk out into the sunshine, your face kind of goes like this (*smiles*), and everybody seems happier.

Between Covid lockdowns, I take a train to a seaside town to write. The early autumn seems absurdly, inappropriately, benign, but it's churlish to resist the welcome of the golden air.

> Covid rising.
> R number, cases and deaths.
> A dragonfly flits
> over next door's kitchen roof.
> Pigeons coo and apples fall
> onto the sun-warmed grass.
> I take off socks, walk barefoot.
> May this too become
> love's instrument.[93]

CREATIVE EXPLORATION

Move – or imagine moving – your body in a way that expresses metta in this moment.
    How about a dance?

(Un)friendly reminders

Community, connection, and relationship are the testing grounds for befriending. The long-term art of befriending includes reconciling with the absence of friendliness as well as its complete opposites.

Unfriendliness is where we learn friendliness. How can the intention of metta be brought into situations of ill will, anger, conflict with others? Can we know these states as they are, and be unafraid to look them in the eye, acknowledge them, and offer care?

Jaya reflects on what has helped:

> Having friends who are wise and kind and who treat me with kindness, modelling a way I can become wiser and kinder towards myself. Metta is learned from the company of good friends, corroborating what the Buddha said about friendship as one of the most important things for the development of our practice. Teaching mindful self-compassion helped me because you have to practise and embody it while you're teaching. The course emphasizes soothing touch, physically holding oneself with kindness. In guided loving-kindness meditations, when teachers used to say, 'You could put a hand on your heart or belly', I found it a bit cheesy, but I've come to realize how helpful physical reassurance is.

In situations where harm and injustice have been perpetrated, care is needed not to force befriending, or to brush aside anger or grief. There can be outer and inner pressures to forgive another for the harm they have caused; some approaches lean in this direction, but it's important that this doesn't result in bypassing or denial of suffering. An attitude of metta does not mean liking or condoning harmful behaviour. Thanissaro Bhikkhu highlights how forgiving another does not mean having to like them, whereas reconciliation means a return to amicability and requires the re-establishing of trust.[94] Mpho Tutu emphasizes the steps needed:

Truth and reconciliation depend on the willingness of both sides to engage. As human beings we actually engage in processes of truth and reconciliation on a daily basis within our own households; we have to live and forgive and reconfigure ourselves over and over again in order to survive as humanity on any level. In a place where racism continues, where the harms continue to be perpetrated, we still engage in the process, we go as far as we can go with it, which is that we tell the truth as much as we can tell the truth, we tell our stories, we explain what the impact of the action is on us. You can't get to forgiveness without confronting the reality of what's happened, you must name the hurt, saying 'This is how I have been injured.' It's not cheap, it's not forgive and forget. You have to actually remember in order to forgive.[95]

I ask Jaya for her reflections on this theme.

I think the biggest difficulty for me is around forgiveness. When there's been a lot of hurt in a relationship, it's very hard to fully forgive and inhabit a space of metta. Rather than demand that one must have metta for an individual that one doesn't feel ready to forgive, it's more helpful to see if one can turn towards the entire situation and constellation of relationships with metta.

CREATIVE EXPLORATION

Contemplate a relationship that is usually straightforward but feels difficult or strained at the moment. Widen your awareness to encompass yourself and the other person. Imagine that both of you, and the relationship as a whole, are held with an intention of goodwill and ease. Soften any tendencies to blame the other or yourself.

What happens?

Metta and everything

Sometimes it seems that everything is conspiring to get in the way of metta. If only that irritating, annoying, hateful... behaviour, politician, circumstance, colleague, weather, mood... would go away, all would be well. Then we remember an intention to practise metta, feel we have fallen short, and get annoyed at ourselves, thus firing another arrow into the already annoyed wound. It's easy to forget how to pause and mentally step back at this point. How is it to bring metta to the irritation, the anger, or the resentment, knowing it as it is, recognizing its shape and form? Hello, it's you again old friend, I see you're in need of some attention. Usually, the attention needed is less than we anticipate. Just the potent courtesy of acknowledgement. Dwelling with what feels hostile – internally or externally – with an intention of metta can soften it and reduce the charge. Little by little the barriers can be broken down, with the intention of heading towards impartiality and unconditionality. Not in the service of repression, or of avoiding any necessary action, but in the service of releasing the heart, and altering future pathways of resentful thoughts, words, and actions.

Extending this, we can play with metta, blending it into moments of contact with mind-states, beings and all that is sensed, whether pleasant, unpleasant, or neither. Noticing that turning towards and becoming interested in what usually feels neutral or is disregarded, such as breath, ground, space, can often change it into something vivid, nourishing, and alive.

Language carves up and makes distinctions that we can creatively undo. Giving, wishing, or offering metta 'to' or 'for' oneself or another creates a certain distancing and objectifying. It can obscure ways in which cultivating the brahma-viharas can increasingly move towards something seamlessly and intrinsically lived. Metta *and* the lower back, the hands, the keyboard, the cup of tea... metta and the carpet, the door handle, the digestion, the absence of metta, the window, the passing car, the birdsong, the interruption, the clouds and on and on...

With your mind imbued with metta, dwell having pervaded one direction, and in the same way the second, the third, and the fourth direction, and also the four intermediate directions, above and below, completely and everywhere. Being without mental shackles, resentment, ill will, or contention, with a mind imbued with metta that is supremely vast and great, boundless and well cultivated, dwell pervading the entire world.[96]

CREATIVE EXPLORATION

Bring attention to the dimension of space – the space around you, within your body, inside and outside the room, the wide space of the sky. Sense or imagine how this might be imbued with, saturated, full of metta. As you breathe in and out, so metta breathes in and out of you.

Phrases and categories

Buddhaghosa's method for practising the brahma-viharas has influenced the ways in which they are practised today. Using the categories of oneself, a benefactor, a dear friend, a neutral person, and a hostile or difficult person, one gradually extends metta (and compassion, joy, equanimity) to all beings everywhere. Repeated phrases bring silent anchors to the mind, returning again and again to good wishes such as 'May you be healthy and well, may you be safe from harm, may you be filled with loving-kindness, may you live with ease.' This systematic breakdown of the practice can be a helpful antidote to distraction, or a skilful approach for minds and hearts that respond well to structure. But it can bind us to habits. After months of imagining the same person in the 'difficult' category, I realized this was cementing hostility rather than easing it. When meeting them I had conditioned myself to anticipate difficulty, rather than allowing the present-moment encounter to be different, and letting in greater fluidity of perception.

Finding an embodied connection with categories or phrases was challenging until I could practise them on a longer retreat. The clarity and steadiness that arose from weeks of silence and simplicity meant the psychophysical system had more stability and could taste the beauty of repetition. When our conversation turns towards traditional forms of metta practice, I learn that Jaya's experience is similar:

> I bought the idea of reciting phrases or returning the mind to a thought or intention, but I've always found it easy to drift off, and feel disconnected from that felt sense of friendliness. It took about thirty-five years before I sat a six-week retreat doing metta practice using the traditional *Visuddhimagga*-style phrases. I would not have enjoyed it or had access to it at the beginning of my practice. Even though we're encouraged (for good reasons) to recognize that metta is an intention, not an emotion or feeling, it's much more fun to practise when intention and felt sense are aligned with one another.

Despite this, even in the turmoil of daily life, repeating phrases can be supportive and grounding. When a line of song gets stuck on repeat in the middle of an activity I enjoy, such as cooking or gardening, I explore replacing it with 'May all beings be well', sometimes to my own tune. The repetition functions as a reminder to consider the welfare of other beings in the vicinity – the slugs in the lettuce, the creatures in the soil, the neighbour across the fence.

Crafting your own phrases can be a delightful development of metta practice. The first phrases I read were in *A Path with Heart* by Jack Kornfield. I learned them diligently, repeating them until they lost their vibrancy, and the main satisfaction was in feeling smug that I had memorized them so well. There are many wonderful suggestions and templates for metta and brahma-vihara phrases. In *Mindful of Race*, Ruth King includes

> May all beings live with an open heart.
> May all beings know joy and freedom.
> May all beings have food, shelter, and good care.
> May all beings be free from animosity and hatred.
> May all beings know peace.
> May all beings be good friends to each other.[97]

In *Lovingkindness* Sharon Salzberg suggests the classical phrases

> May I be free from danger.
> May I have mental and physical happiness.
> May I have ease of well-being.[98]

In *Boundless Heart* Christina Feldman accentuates the importance of 'befriending the mind of the moment', planting seeds of intention in the midst of everything:

> May I be safe and well in the midst of all things.
> May I be peaceful in the midst of all moments.
> May I abide in ease and in kindness.[99]

Phrases can be shortened into a simple word or image dropped into awareness and spread in all directions like the ripples of a pebble thrown into a lake: warmth, contentment, nourishment. Like each of us, all beings face uncertainty and change, hope and despair, pain and loss, as well as success, happiness, and ease. Remembering and deeply internalizing this awareness can be the starting point for creating phrases. Take time to consider the conditions that all forms of life wish for and need to flourish, and weave them into your own words.

CREATIVE EXPLORATION

During your next activity drop a metta phrase into the mind,
such as 'May all beings be well', or develop your own words and phrases.
Running a tap, brushing your teeth, putting on a coat, opening the door... may
we be healthy, may we live in peace.

Notice what the effect is, the moments when it feels genuine, the moments
when it becomes mechanical.

Metta and compassion

When metta encounters suffering and stays loving, it becomes
compassion. Drawing on the imagery of a vast mycelial web, a deep
well endlessly replenished, or a big sky, metta can transform into
soothing for overwhelm and a balm for burnout. My conversation with
Jaya draws to a close with an acknowledgement of conditions in the
world around us:

> We live in a toxic culture in terms of public discourse. The level
> of hate that people express has become almost normal, and
> unfortunately a number of people act on it. If metta were more
> highly praised, much harm could be avoided, and a lot of healing
> could happen. There's mindfulness in Parliament and in schools,
> maybe there could be metta too. Metta is essential in enabling a
> compassionate response to ever-increasing suffering.
>
> One must be resourced to translate compassionate intention
> into compassionate action. Generosity with our energy, time,
> and resources is called for, and generosity is metta in action.
> Another expression is the commitment to restraining harmful
> impulses, commitment to truthfulness, to non-greed, to not taking
> things when they're not freely given. All these are kindness and
> compassion in and of themselves.
>
> We need activists in the world, but there are lots of things
> we can do that aren't about being an activist 'out there'. Setting

boundaries on one's behaviours and patterns of consumption is also compassionate action, with potentially world-changing results.

There's a passage in the *Metta Sutta*: 'Let none deceive another or despise any being in any state'; 'despise' really means 'ignore'. This is metta and compassion eliding into each other. Being interested in the plight of other beings, not seeing them as irrelevant. Metta as open-eyed and curious and caring.

CREATIVE EXPLORATION

Consciously engage in a simple action with the intention of kindness, towards yourself, others, or both. What effect does this have?

Chapter 3
ENJOYING

Whatever one frequently thinks about and considers becomes the inclination of one's heart.

Two Kinds of Thought Sutta[100]

The full range

What does joy mean to you? Are you for it, against it, or on the fence? Take a moment to pause and let your responses surface.

Joy doesn't have to be bells and whistles, all-singing, all-dancing. The experience of joy is usually marked by simplicity. It could include a moment of letting go of tasks, resting back, noticing the play of light on a wall, the sound of birdsong or passing traffic. It extends to absorbing and delighting in nature, or enjoying contact with other beings, human and non-human. Moments of lingering and dwelling with what feels okay, good, or pleasant. It encompasses the subtle joy of recognizing the way things are, even the acknowledgement of joy's opposites: envy, discontent, gloom. It has a vast range. When cultivated and developed it includes gratitude, generosity, delight in the good fortune and happiness of others. It includes contentment. Increasing our capacity to notice and take in what is well is an essential support for compassion. We are conditioned to search for external sources of happiness. There is profound pressure to find and retain these. We look for lasting satisfaction in romantic relationships, a delicious meal, work success, a fabulous holiday, better knowledge, new skills, validation from others. Worth is often measured against whether, and how quickly, we can acquire these and how well we match up to our peers' and society's expectations. There is nothing wrong with the enjoyment that these bring. The human longing for novelty fuels exploration, art, and science. But every experience, no matter how enjoyable, sooner or later ends. Nothing external brings permanent contentment. In the cultural imperatives of the late capitalist era, once one longing finishes it is often replaced with a new longing. When we begin to see through the pressure this exerts, there's a double whammy: we berate ourselves for being caught again, and we long for the end of longing.

The compulsion to find lasting happiness through what we produce or consume can fuel boundless insatiability and, at its extreme end, addiction. One Christmas I received a box of chocolates; I was pleased, I like chocolate. Under the logo was the strapline 'You choose the moment. We'll provide the bliss.' The first one was outstanding, melt-in-the-mouth scrumptious. The impact on my tastebuds lasted seconds. The urge to eat another was immediate and irresistible. The ability to 'choose' to obey this urge or not quickly vanished. Is this bliss?

When we encounter meditation practice, what can leap out at first is an emphasis on reducing stress and finding a calmer, less reactive relationship to our experience. This can be combined with an apparent condemnation of desire, which we quickly turn into an assumption that any kind of enjoyment is trouble. In fact, the capacity for gladdening the mind and heart is central in Buddhist teachings. It includes the bliss of refraining from doing harm, the delight of seclusion, the joy of gathering awareness in meditative absorption so that the mind unifies and releases into profound peace. The spectrum of joy is not a denial of difficulty, but a wellspring of agency, empowerment, and freedom. Exploring and cultivating this resource helps develop a capacity to bear what is difficult, through patiently disentangling from habit patterns that don't serve us, and discovering the pathways that lead to greater contentment. Turning attention to what is well supports us to meet and respond to stress and unpredictability. Longchenpa's poem quoted in the introduction offers the image of compassion watered by joy's tears. Without joy, compassion becomes brittle, lifeless, and unsustainable.

Blackbird
eating red berries
on hawthorn;
why this joy? these tears?
why ask the question?[101]

What does joy mean to you?

How do you recognize joy or gladness?

Opening the heart

I met Kareem Ghandour when we were on the staff team at an iBme mindfulness retreat for teenagers.[102] In a twice-daily group with other adults who were first-time mentors, we were guided through the icebreakers, games, and heart-opening practices that teens themselves experience in these groups. The sharings are often profound, sometimes hilarious, a unique and memorable way of connecting. In creative workshops the young people worked with Kareem and me to write a song for the final night's community share, and, from a disparate collection of instruments, tunes, words, and ideas, something playful, celebratory, and magical emerged.

Kareem is of Palestinian and Lebanese heritage and grew up in Jordan. His father was a Zen practitioner, but Kareem did not explore meditation until he began to struggle with alcohol and depression as a teenager. As a young adult he travelled to Plum Village in France, the community centred on the teachings of Vietnamese Zen master Thich Nhat Hanh (known as Thay). He has since spent many years engaged in mindfulness education, and trained as a mindfulness teacher with Jack Kornfield and Tara Brach.

Through the bonding of the iBme community, Kareem has become a friend, and it was truly enjoyable to have a conversation about a theme dear to our hearts. He describes his first encounter with joy as a spiritual practice:

> I showed up at Plum Village knowing nothing about Thich Nhat Hanh's philosophy or teaching. I went there to keep deepening

peace and have support of a *sangha*. 'OK,' I thought, 'I'm going to meditate and that's it.'

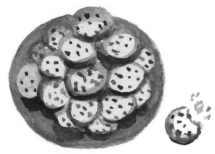

There was a Christmas Eve gathering, they call them be-ins; I felt quite armoured because it was all a bit cheesy. Cookies were passed around; we were singing carols and there were candles. Then I felt this overwhelming warmth and a very innocent childlike joy popped up. It was a huge heart-opening, not just emotionally healing, but something very pure. All the hard layers fell away, I was in tears; I realized, 'Wow, I'm here singing all these Christmas songs!' Something about that experience infused my practice from then on.

Even though I came back to university in the UK, and the conditions weren't all that wholesome, meditation practice was like returning to this natural state, a sense of wonder, of touching a purer intention. Because I continued with Thay's teachings, meditation was about the magic of being alive. Joy as a centrepiece informed my whole practice.

Kareem's experience shows how joy can be sparked by conditions, by connection and beauty, how it can live underground until a door opens, and then shock us with its sudden emergence. I picture Kareem, and some of the things I know about him – his dedication to empowering youth and building community, his playfulness, sensitivity, and generosity, his love of heavy-metal band Tool, his beloved cat Gaia – and imagine his heart opening amidst cookies, carols, and candlelight, and, well, it brings me great joy too.

CREATIVE EXPLORATION

Imagine, remember, or act from a place of joyful silliness, light-heartedness or playfulness. Doodle, shimmy, make a face, sing... What's it like to take yourself less seriously?

Backdraught

[noun] *A rapid or explosive burning of superheated gases, caused when oxygen enters an oxygen-depleted environment.*

Turning towards joy can invoke its opposites. Is cynicism, sadness, irritation, or even fury arising as you read these paragraphs? Such responses are a natural part of this landscape and are sometimes the result of being conditioned to perceive only the downsides and negatives, a suspicion towards noticing goodness and what is well.

Cultivating gladness does not need to involve repressing our objections to it. If we try to ignore resistance, the process of uncovering joy will become dishonest and shallow. There can also be strong cultural messages to pretend all is well when it clearly isn't. As a young woman waking up to sexism and determined not to 'smile and be nice', I was the target of comments from men I passed in the street:

'Cheer up, it may never happen!'

'When the wind changes you'll stay like that!'

Needless to say, these deepened my rage.

Cultivating joy doesn't give immunity from anger, heartbreak, or fear; it doesn't deny that these are sometimes necessary and appropriate responses. It does offer a stepping-stone to surface out of confusion, turn towards these feelings in an embodied way, let them in, and learn to respond wisely. Allowing greater ease in mind and body supports us to act with care for ourselves and others, not through the pressure of social or cultural expectations but because this response leads onwards to greater freedom.

We may arrive at the door of meditation or mindfulness with a hidden, or not so hidden, agenda of creating a better version of ourselves, an undertaking that is often a joy-depleted environment. Tara Brach's description of this state as 'the trance of unworthiness' captures its unconscious nature.[103] When we're in this trance, any discernment is blotted out. The trance appears solid, real. It *is* the truth. We can't tell that it is being woven and rewoven by inner monologues of unworthiness, because our entire perspective has these beliefs imprinted through it like the lettering in a stick of seaside rock. Only after emerging from the trance can we see how we've been caught in its fog.

Peeling back layers of unworthiness to receive the subtle comfort of delight takes time and patience. We may encounter waves of depression. We may reach a certain level of acceptance and think we've gone as far as we can, only to find that relationship challenges, work stress, health crises reveal new territories where tendencies for self-blame and punishment hold sway. The poet Mary Oliver tenderly invites us to incline again and again towards a glad soothing for our minds and hearts: 'let the soft animal of your body / love what it loves.'[104]

I ask Kareem about the obstacles he has encountered:

Joy is fragile sometimes and needs protection and tending. If I just let the mind rip, if I don't water the seeds of joy, and show up for myself, actively do stuff out of self-love, it becomes harder and harder for joy to grow, and makes the practice diminish in terms of energy and embodiment. Another obstacle is being attached to it. Because I have such a meaningful relationship to joy, I can still fear and resist depression and low states. It doesn't serve to hold too tightly to the joy, better to be able to let it go and be a bit more organic. Sometimes I've been scared to experience more unsettledness, thinking that I'm going to lose joy for good. There's a clinging that comes from fear of losing it.

'Self-care' has become a twenty-first-century meme that is sometimes disconnected from real care. It can pull us in conflicting directions: towards the beguiling promises of the wellness industry, or towards an endless self-improvement project. The path of cultivating joy does not deny the felt sense of a self fully deserving of love, care, and joy, and it offers a view of this as a process, constantly in motion, dependent on myriad conditions, full of possibility and mystery. This view is not a negation, but a way of relating that liberates perception and frees us to take ourselves more lightly.

> The swifts are back,
> early morning, feathers rustle
> as one enters the eaves' nest.
> I sit in bed and watch
> four sculpt the day.
> Whose joy –
> theirs-mine-theirs?[105]

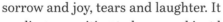

CREATIVE EXPLORATION

Turning towards happiness and joy can raise memories of surviving trauma, neglect, or lack of care. Be respectful of yourself as you engage with this section. Find support from a friend or mentor if need be.

What happens when you open to delight or contentment?

Does joy come with conditions? With strings attached?

Tending joy

When we open to what is well, we may open to what is bittersweet. Young leaves emerge along the spring hedgerows, there is beauty and fresh hope in their soft greenness, and there is vulnerability – a late frost may wither them. Sometimes gladness lies on the cusp of sorrow and joy, tears and laughter. It lingers waiting to be sensed just beyond the preoccupations that keep us from being intimate with and awakened by life as it flows and ebbs, in us and around us. When we find the key of joy and build access to a fuller range of feeling, it broadens our perspective and helps discern how best to respond to ourselves and others. Opening to joy also enables us to find humour without deprecation, and to take life more lightly. To not sink into despair or be defined by it. At iBme retreats, another highlight of the community share is fellow mentor Martina's stand-up routine of mindfulness and meditation jokes, including this one: 'What does a meditator say when they order a pizza? Make me one with everything!'

How do we tend and gladden the heart amid challenges? Not as denial of pain, or as a pitstop refuel so we can continue towards burnout, but as a radical resourcing. Jack Kornfield writes: 'In joy we're not afraid of pleasure, we do not mistakenly believe it's disloyal to the suffering of the world to honour the happiness we've been given.'[106]

Sometimes we can prime and reboot gladness through the example or support of others. Not by objectifying but by being inspired. We look at role models and fantasize that they pull everything out of thin air, but then recall the practice, friends, and communities that sustain them and are not immediately visible. A field of flowers in bloom or the lush shade of a tree in full leaf makes our hearts sing; this blossoming is made possible by roots working deep into the soil and the nourishment of earth, sun, air, and water.

Kareem shares some of the things that help him remember how to tend joy:

> I love walking meditation as a way of connecting, nourishing myself from sensory experience and the natural world. I tend to take whatever I'm enjoying and make it a practice; one thing that's consistent is tea meditation, the pleasant sensations and wellness that come from drinking good tea in a meditative way, savouring that but then letting it drip into the practice, helping it move along. These days I do a lot more music meditation, not playing but listening to a track. In the autumn and winter I tend to feel shut down, and it helps to sit on my cushion and play a song and help it revive my energy. Taking whatever I love and appreciate, and making it a practice and ritual that then supports mindfulness to grow and deepen.

Drinking tea with Kareem, the ritual of selecting the leaves, steeping, pouring, sipping, reminds me of the joy of doing one thing at a time. The radical act of ignoring the infinite To-Do lists. The sublime gift of undivided attention.

CREATIVE EXPLORATION

 Guided Meditation – Enjoying

What is well? Here, now, in a fleeting moment of sensation – light, sound, colour, texture, taste, image. Can you linger with what delights you for a few moments longer?

What simple daily activities can support you to connect with and tend joy?

Envy

A common feature of the brahma-viharas is that they are relational, and the classical understanding of joy is as appreciative, empathic, and altruistic joy, happiness for the happiness of others, joy without self-interest. When we are conditioned by competition and scarcity, an ability to take genuine delight in the good fortune of others is a challenge, a profound antidote to jealousy, and an inexhaustible source of gladness.

Like the dwelling places of metta, compassion, and equanimity, mudita or appreciative joy is an art and craft, it takes time to establish. To be sincere, it needs to be built on foundations of patience, forgiveness, and friendliness towards ourselves. Rejoicing in another's joy can be counter-cultural, going against the torrent of comparison, criticism, and ranking, a deluge magnified by social media. Appreciative joy is an immense resource for those who can give and receive it. Recall the occasions when you have felt wholehearted delight from others for an achievement or success. These instances can be rare jewels. If unused to unconditional approval, we question and find ways to undermine it. Receiving an unexpected bursary, when the giver told me of the gift with visible delight and wished me 'Great joy on the path!', I recoiled slightly, suspicious of their motivation. There was no landing place for this altruistic joy.

Kareem and I discuss the role of sympathetic joy and its connection with spiritual friendship:

> Thay is all about 'Let's just call it joy, because joy is joy!' Delighting in someone's good fortune or being happy that they're happy is such a deep practice, I'm inspired to cultivate it, beyond the people it's easy to do it for. The more joy I can touch, the easier it is to feel for others; it's much harder if reserves are low. Another way sympathetic joy manifests is when sharing practice spaces with others, seeing their goodness, and having that spiritual friendship. That's the way I like to connect with it, rather than just being happy for someone's good news. Of course, there's jealousy sometimes, but working with practitioner friends or being in sangha with them, there's something deeply nourishing and beautiful about taking time to appreciate someone else's good qualities and rejoicing in them. There's a Plum Village tradition called Flower Watering, where we share another's good qualities with them, and it's beautiful to name them.

Even amid great suffering – collective or individual – there can be success, happiness, good fortune. How do we recognize and absorb this as fully as we recognize and absorb all that is not well? Can we encounter the inevitable worldly winds of praise and blame, success and failure, gain and loss, pleasure and pain, without either side cancelling each other out? The neuroscientist and long-term meditator Rick Hanson describes the enduring effect of negativity bias, a side-effect of evolution in surviving hazards, predators, and aggression from other species: 'the brain is like Velcro for negative experiences, but Teflon for positive ones.'[107]

Jealousy and envy are easier to perceive in others than in ourselves. These are painful states to acknowledge, often buried in shame. I watch my niece and nephew navigating the ups and downs of a sibling relationship. The younger innocently takes hold of her brother's toy, and he becomes incensed, yells at her, bursts into tears. Anyone who spends time with children knows the pain fuelled by perceived inequality or injustice. As adults we (mostly) learn to disguise or suppress these feelings, rather than shouting 'That's *mine!*' We hide behind a forced smile or social-media 'likes' for sumptuous meals or stunning holiday photos. Jealousy burns strongly when someone else gets what we'd hoped for. A friend confesses that, after years of genuinely liking a friend's Instagram feed, the first time they post a success that she also wants, she is awash with envy, even more shocking because it had never occurred to her to want it.

Inclining towards appreciative joy is a practice; it might feel awkward at first, like learning musical scales before progressing to playing tunes. We can begin by pausing, tuning to the ground, to metta and the body, taking small steps, which may not always go forwards. Noticing momentary delights in others' lives – the single-mindedness of birds building their nests, the sound of neighbours chatting, a stranger who wishes us a cheery 'Good morning' as we pass them in the street.

Joy is an antidote to guilt, to shame at having fortunate circumstances when many are struggling. Taking full permission to enjoy and absorb what is well resources us, and this is a gift to others. In November 2020, as the world held its breath awaiting the outcome of the US election, in between news bulletins I caught a nature programme about the phenomenon of mast years, when trees simultaneously produce a bumper crop of seeds and nuts, ensuring the success of their future generations, and providing a welcome harvest for birds and animals.

> A simple joy slips into finger-holds and crevices
> and builds from many sources – long-tailed tits
> wittering in silver birch, clusters of nitrous
> bonnet-caps, a beech limb rippling
> with curtain fungus, light filtered
> through a lacy canopy – I let it grow,
> keep out the news, keep in new knowledge
> that the acorns underfoot are raining down
> from oak trees everywhere. Plentiful. A mast year.[108]

CREATIVE EXPLORATION

Think of someone you know who has had success or good news recently. It's easier if the source of their happiness is not something you also wish for, but you can try this too. Notice the responses that arrive. If there is any flavour of delight, stay with it for a while. Offer your wishes that their happiness and good fortune continue, and increase... What do you notice?

Coming home to yourself

Finding joy in community and spaces of shared identity, I relish being out, proud, loud, and enjoying others take this space. Food and medicine for the heart. These spaces can also be edgy. The prospect and promise of belonging can awaken memories of not belonging. Coming out as a young lesbian, there seemed to be many unspoken rules; breaking them felt inevitable. Was there a place for longing, ambivalence, contradictions, and questions?

Listening to others has shown me that these dilemmas are human; it's not unusual to feel like an outsider, wanting to fit in but suspicious of those who do. A blessing of age is less concern about conforming, enjoying a trust in belonging, not from external permission, but from silently touching the earth, as the Buddha did in response to Mara's 'Who do you think you are?' and affirming the expression of life that is *this* life.

Kareem shares the impact of finding joy and empowerment in affinity spaces:

> Expressing and embodying joy is a reconnection to my heritage. Both my cultures tend to be expressive on both ends, so when there's suffering and grief it's felt and expressed deeply, and when there's joy it's also passionate. Being a 'serene meditator' in the Zen tradition cut me off from that ancestral life force, and how I am generally as a person.
>
> When I first attended people of colour practice communities, and saw different expressions of Dharma, I noticed how there had been cultural assimilation. I'd thought it was good practice to be reserved in a certain way, that that's what being mindful should look like. I'd internalized a message of 'Those Arabs, they're just too over-the-top, they don't intersect with Dharma practice.' It's a somatic experience to be around black and brown people and people of colour and to see how practice is expressed through their bodies, their ways of talking, the way they celebrate. I was able to touch that on a deeper level, in a very bodily way, and that's what made my practice authentic, reclaiming the fullness of who I am.

In BIPOC groups, when I'm designing sessions or holding a space, the joy and celebration and creativity and music are abundant. They tend to be characteristics of BIPOC spaces: let's see how we want to celebrate, let's create our own table. Not to dishonour the form, but how can we experiment? What's our creative way of honouring ourselves? Of honouring ancestors, of celebrating being in community? Taking refuge also in the resilient joy of ancestors, that's something so meaningful to connect with.

When I go back home I see how much suffering there is, but that people can really show up with joy together. People can be feeling miserable in their individual lives, but they know how to bring happiness when they gather together. There's just a default that we're going to rejoice in each other and have a great time. We know how to switch the dial.

After the first or second BIPOC retreat, I noticed I was walking differently. It touches something greater than joy, of course, but joy is part of that empowerment. I felt more upright in my spine, somatically morphing into something more expansive and whole. I imagine it's the same for other affinity spaces too, feeling like you're coming home to yourself.

It's important to honour our different doors and pathways to joy. We all have our own unique flavour and inclination, so it's an exploration and we shouldn't limit ourselves, finding our own joy ingredients, cooking them up in a big pot.

CREATIVE EXPLORATION

Recall a time when you felt at home in yourself. Perhaps with friends or community, or in a location that is easeful and comforting, and gives a sense of belonging. Bring attention to the felt sensations in the body. Stay a while with what feels good.

Joy in the midst

Lockdown temporarily lifted, a sunny autumn afternoon, a city park. We take off our masks, sit on the grass, awkward after months on Zoom or phone.

'Bow' is the co-founder of a support group for lesbian, bisexual, and trans women who seek refuge in the UK:

> What I remember about that day was how much fun it was to play dodgeball. It reminded me of being a girl. I haven't been home for the longest time, and playing took me back home and brought back happy childhood memories. We would stack up flat stones in the middle to mark who was winning. If you dodged the ball, then you put a stone on the stack and scored a point.[109]

Olu arrives unexpectedly – it's Nigerian Independence Day and she's driven here on her day off from frontline health care, with trays of chicken, jollof rice, and roasted vegetables. Smiles blossom, shyness dissipates. Soon there's laughter at the dodgeball hits and misses, the double-bluffing.

> It unified us. We were all happy to be out of the house, happy to see each other. It was great to hear people talking about playing dodgeball in childhood. I didn't know it was a common thing in other African countries.

A break for mango juice and G gets out her phone to play a video of *Jerusalema*, the song and dance craze from South Africa that has taken the pandemic-riven world by storm. Everyone tries to copy the steps, falling over, turning the wrong way, singing, laughing.

Times like these take away the stress of thinking about your situation. It reminds us that we are people, playful people, people with lives apart from the asylum system. It makes you authentic, the real you. When you are in the system nobody can see your potential or your fun side. Times like these mean that for a few hours you don't have to think about not having your papers. It puts you in a different space. I never knew what depression was until I came to this country.

I think about my mum giving birth to me and giving me my name. This is you, there is nothing else. Then life comes in and a lot of things change; you are tagged, you become this or that, so many tags, it's crazy. A day like this gives you space, gives you freedom for a while. It makes you human again.

Gratitude

The jostling and scraping pause as we line up in school uniform along the tables. The teacher bows her head and begins to intone grace. We join in, mumbling and impatient, willing away these seconds until we can yank out our chairs and start gobbling shepherd's pie.

'For what we are about to receive may the Lord make us truly grateful.'

For my parents, the sight of bananas or oranges evoked memories of rationing in the Second World War, and elicited reminders of how fortunate we, their children, were to enjoy such things. As a young adult I received gifts with embarrassment, an immediate urge to return the generosity, to outdo the giver. Simply receiving without reciprocation was a cause for shame.

When consciously cultivating joy became a practice, some of the habits generated by past experience revealed themselves. I learned to feel gratitude without guilt, to taste the 'joy for oneself' that is a definition of gratitude.

In positive psychology research, the practice of gratitude has been shown to have significant benefits. It is associated with better physical and psychological health, greater happiness and life satisfaction, less materialism. Gratitude is shown to inspire generosity and prosocial behaviour, to strengthen relationships, and improve the climate in workplaces.[110]

One study uncovered cultural differences: people in the UK more frequently reported that gratitude is linked with various negative emotions including guilt, indebtedness, embarrassment, and awkwardness than did people in the United States.[111]

There is also evidence that gratitude has significant downsides. People with disabilities who relied on informal support for their care often felt burdened by gratitude, and reported feeling forced to express gratitude to secure the support they needed, expressing shame and frustration over the one-sided nature of their dependent relationships. In contrast, people with disabilities who were able to pay for formal support reported feeling more comfortable and more in control of their lives.[112]

Gratitude, while helping to form and maintain relationships, may sometimes play a nefarious role in them. In situations of inequity, 'a lack of gratitude may be a more moral response', writes Liz Jackson. She continues:

> Promoting propositional gratitude to disadvantaged people of color in the United States, to manual laborers, people in abusive partnerships or children in bad family situations may benefit the individual or people psychologically and instrumentally. Yet it may lead as well to denial of challenges faced, or irrational minimization of problems, when suggested as a coping mechanism or everyday practice across such contexts.[113]

These undercurrents warrant careful consideration, and research methodologies may have biases that obscure the experience of disabled people and people of colour, as has been shown in terms of gender.[114] More work is needed on how gratitude affects compassion fatigue and empathic distress, but the study quoted above does show that, in the context of reducing stress and alleviating burnout, teachers and health-care practitioners who counted their blessings over a four- or eight-week period experienced a greater sense of accomplishment, a decline in symptoms of depression, and less emotional exhaustion.[115]

Gratitude, like joy, can raise memories of lack, or be misused to paper over harm and injustice. It requires nuance. And, when we focus on acts of giving and receiving, we may forget the Dharma perspective of non-separation. As we'll see in Chapter 4, sustaining compassion points us towards the constancy of interconnection: the flow of caring in which there is no giver, no receiver.

CREATIVE EXPLORATION

What are you grateful for in this moment? What helps you to wholeheartedly receive it? Make a note, on paper, phone, through any medium, or just in your head. Repeat this for a few days and notice the effects.

Generosity

The Book of Joy documents an astonishing week that Archbishop Desmond Tutu and His Holiness the Dalai Lama spent together in Dharamsala, exploring joy in the face of suffering. Their affection for each other, their delight in each other's company, and the wisdom gained from finding compassion amid great hardship brim into every moment of the encounter. Asked about how to find joy in life when so many are in pain, Archbishop Tutu replies:

> Hey, remember you are not alone, and you do not need to finish the work. It takes time, but we are learning, we are growing, we are becoming the people we want to be. It helps no one if you sacrifice your joy because others are suffering. We people who care must be attractive, must be filled with joy, so that others recognize that caring, that helping and being generous are not a burden, they are a joy. Give the world your love, your service, your healing, but you can also give it your joy. This, too, is a great gift.[116]

Generosity can sit very differently with us, depending on the cultures and values in which we've been raised and educated. Have you been taught or advised to give at arm's length, to be careful of someone taking advantage of you? Or to give unstintingly without any thought for your own wellbeing? Do you give hoping that something will return? Do you give hoping that others will notice and think better of you? Generosity comes with multiple shapes, forms, and motivations.

Generosity need not be material; it includes wholehearted attention, unconditional listening, the gift of presence and witnessing. In the act of giving, there is the potential to make connection with another; when we connect, we reach out from the confines of our own interests, and – for a moment or for longer – can be shaken from our habitual perspectives.

Giving can therefore become a foundation for cultivating joy, contentment, and freedom, a support for dissolving comparisons.

Kareem draws together the threads of generosity, happiness, and the sacred:

> The way I relate to joy has expanded a lot since I first went to Plum Village: there's a sense of wellbeing and energy that takes many forms. It can be quite content and calm, but I also relate to it as a life force that I need to keep feeding to be engaged and connected. It's not just about being happy, it's about a basic sense of being resourced, having energy to meet the great and the difficult. From a spiritual perspective there's a connection to the sacred too, a quality of reverence. I notice when I appreciate something or connect with it more intimately, there's a sense in the heart, a sense of sacred that opens. It can expand a sense of care and of wanting to protect things.

CREATIVE EXPLORATION

Remember a time when you felt ungenerous. What do you notice in your mind and body?

What happens when there is an intention towards giving?

How can you be generous in this moment?

Kindling for compassion

Why is joy important in the service of compassion? When I ask Kareem this question, he has no doubts that joy is a door to the other brahma-viharas:

> Joy is like the first step, an easy springboard to all of them. Energy and interest and some degree of enthusiasm, I need those ingredients for compassion to come, and to be able to turn towards something more difficult. Showing up for another, energy to receive it properly, not get burned by the difficult, you need enough resource to do that. If I build that reserve of wellbeing more regularly, that can convert into compassion for a difficult situation. Otherwise in difficult places it's too dark. Compassion doesn't come first, there must be some other kind of light and wellbeing, then this gives kindling for compassion.

We speak about the meaning of joy in the most challenging of situations, and Kareem reflects on his work with young people:

> I connect with the idea, practice, and aspiration of offering joy to other people as an engaged practice. I think that's overlooked, because we think of compassion and kindness as the ones that are offered out, but showing up with joy is a beautiful gift, it's another kind of love. Showing up with wellbeing, with resource, with aliveness has a beautiful impact. That's the main ingredient in the bag when I teach youth, and the most important thing I have to offer.
>
> From an activism perspective, joy is a medicine to keep going, to actually enjoy the work. I find Palestinian justice stuff so heavy, I can only take a certain dose of news, but if I'm planning for something, I like to see, 'How can I turn towards the light in the experience, the creativity of it, the people I'm working with?' Coming from the enjoyment and the care, there's inspiration. Even though there's lots of despair, and the Israeli Occupation, there's a happiness in doing something about it. Riding that energy is quite sustainable, the heaviness doesn't have long fuel and doesn't put out the good energy.

CREATIVE EXPLORATION

Bring awareness to an intention or action to care or be of service (including to yourself). It could be simply preparing a meal or cup of tea, answering an email, listening to a colleague or child, or something more long-term. Can you come to this, as Kareem says, with the intention of enjoyment?
What effect does this have?

Freedom

Joy in itself does not bring an end to dissatisfaction. It is dependent on conditions, but we can learn the pathways that lead towards greater capacity for and openness to joy. We do not have to wait until joy comes knocking, or grab hold as it flits past: we can deliberately and consciously tend and cultivate it. Joy is a resource that helps us look deeply into the nature of things. It supports courage, fearlessness, and stillness. Empathic joy opens the heart, connects us, breaks down the barriers between self and other. Joy can give us the strength to simplify, to let go, to turn towards the impermanent and imperfect nature of all things including ourselves. Facing the truth that we will lose everything we hold dear sounds like a recipe to break the heart, but clinging on only shatters it more comprehensively.

> They that bind to themselves a joy
> Do the wingèd life destroy
> They that kiss the joy as it flies
> Live in eternity's sunrise.

If, as William Blake suggests, we 'kiss the joy as it flies', we can let go into the tenderness of impermanence, feeding a joy in the present moment that then supports the possibility of more letting go.[117]

Just as with the other brahma-viharas, the heavenly realms that stretch beyond our comprehension like stars in a night sky, joy has a boundlessness that reminds us of the unbinding at the heart of the Buddha's teachings. 'Unbound' and 'unfettered' are synonyms for 'awakening', and this connection with infinity is pointed to in Blake's poem, where those who fully meet joy in its transience 'live in eternity's sunrise'.

The five daily recollections of impermanence and mortality are a traditional Buddhist practice. This version is a modern adaptation that has been broadened to include the possibility of living with joy, even alongside acute awareness of change and loss. It can be spoken aloud or silently recalled, perhaps as you gently place a hand on the upper chest or lower belly and feel the rhythm of breath as it comes and goes.

Breathing gently, I lovingly remember
sickness, ageing, and death are part of life,
loss and separation are also unavoidable.
In the light of this, how may I live wisely, joyfully,
and well?

CREATIVE EXPLORATION

Gently enquire 'What is well?' and tune in to any pleasant sensations: a part of the body that feels warm and comfy, a good smell, a pleasing colour. Allow the sensation to expand and spread so that it moves beyond the pleasant feeling-tone and encompasses all things that come into your awareness.

Sustain this with the following phrases:

Enjoying what is well in this moment
Enjoying what is well in this life

And extend it to others nearby:

May you enjoy what is well in this moment
May you enjoy what is well in this life.[118]

Chapter 4
CARING

Compassion is not a thing to accomplish, wrapped as a present, given as a gift, or practiced. It can only boil up in the deepest pain until it spills into the laps of those who surround you. This is the experience of peace in a circle of humanity that lives together rather than one group exploiting another.

Zenju Earthlyn Manuel[119]

Connection

Loneliness is said to be one of the epidemics of our age, particularly in the Global North, where families live in smaller households, many live alone, and there is an ageing demographic. Research by a UK charity shows it is a deep and pervasive current; in 2021, 3.7 million people reported that they were often or always lonely. Though the lockdowns were universal, Covid-19 exacerbated existing inequalities; groups already at risk of loneliness were at greater risk.[120] However, loneliness is not caused only by solitude; another version of it exists in the cramped, overcrowded conditions endured by large families with little accessible public space.

The pandemic magnified the impact of isolation on physical and mental health, and foregrounded the human need for, and dependency on, connection. As it unfolded, we saw acutely how our actions and inactions could protect or risk our own and others' lives, and how dependent we were on frontline workers (who are often the lowest paid). In January 2020, unaware of what the year would bring, I resolved to write a daily poem on the theme of metta. Three months on, as Covid-19 took hold, dependency on others became vivid:

> After several days' absence
> I walk to the lambing field
> and hear the first cuckoo.
>
> In the space between sounds
> I think about human shields:
> nurses, doctors, shelf-stackers,
> delivery drivers.
>
> It's not acceptable
> for a self-respecting poet
> to use the word 'heartbreak'
> yet here it is.[121]

This interdependence or interbeing – a term coined by Thich Nhat Hanh – can be forgotten in the humdrum of daily pressures, obscuring that our lives are sustained by the work, efforts, and lives of other beings. Conditions of relative comfort and protection in the Global North are made possible by restrictions and vulnerability felt by those in the Global South. Other realms of suffering are deliberately kept out of sight or hidden, through industrial and agricultural systems, or the suffering displaced into the future through overshooting the planet's current resources.

Melany Zarate, an indigenous climate activist and land defender from Colombia, expresses a powerful reminder of this:

> It is important to understand how Buddhism can help ease suffering for us – the people who are called to put our bodies on the line to defend water, land, and spirit. ... It must recognize the needs of those communities, really listen to them, and recognize their time with money. ... When you see brave work don't just clap, ask 'How can I support?' Indigenous people protect 80 per cent of the Earth's biodiversity yet they only represent 5 per cent of the population. Centring their voices means protecting us all.[122]

Brave work and conversations benefit from and inspire *kalyana-mittata*, wholesome or spiritual friendship. In April 2019 I met Esther Slattery when she spoke on 'Practising an inclusive Dharma' at a panel chaired by Lama Rod Owens. Esther is a black Londoner, mother of two, mindfulness and yoga teacher, nurse, and psychotherapist, who has practised Buddhist meditation since the 1980s. Her grounded presence and her caring, enquiring character reflect the time she spends in nature, tending her garden and walking in the Lake District and Snowdonia. I value the spiritual companionship that evolves from exploring allyship across identities of race and sexuality. During one of our conversations, Esther describes what embodying compassion means for her:

Compassion is present when you are with somebody who's hurting, and you feel like you're hurting. And that's very different to when I'm watching, and I can see your suffering, but I'm removed. Sometimes it shows up in the room when you hear somebody's story, and you find your whole self responding. There's a sense of being activated, of being moved, and it's not possible to have that distance that sometimes we can hold.

Boundlessness

This innate capacity to be moved and respond with compassion is, when fully cultivated, immeasurable and boundless. Can the beauty of boundlessness have a practical and immediate dimension? Interdependence can't be rationally thought out, just as the boundless dimension of the brahma-viharas cannot be cognitively mapped. The body, heart, and imagination must come online to flesh out and support the concepts of friendliness, joy, or compassion, and the intention to cultivate and offer them unconditionally. In the words of Dr Martin Luther King Jr,

> We are all caught in an inescapable network of mutuality, tied into a single garment of destiny. Whatever affects one directly, affects all indirectly ... before you finish eating breakfast in the morning, you've depended on more than half of the world.[123]

The path towards boundlessness can begin with the immediate, tangible experience of recalling and picturing those whose work has provided the food on our plate. Those who tended and harvested the trees and crops, who transported and refrigerated, who sorted and packed, who lifted and carried, who peeled and chopped. In the *Metta Sutta* goodwill and friendliness are initially directed at particular groups of beings, as if the sutta offers these descriptions to spark imagination.

Whatever living beings there may be,
Whether they are weak or strong, omitting none,
The great or the mighty, medium, short, or small,

The seen and the unseen,
Those living near and far away,
Those born and to-be-born,
May all beings be at ease.

The sutta continues with a more specific image, before broadening out towards boundlessness:

Even as a mother protects with her life
Her child, her only child
So with a boundless heart
Should one cherish all living beings,
Radiating kindness over the entire world:

Spreading upwards to the skies,
And downwards to the depths,
Outwards and unbounded,
Freed from hatred and ill-will.[124]

Although the *Metta Sutta* is primarily concerned with the capacity for goodwill and friendliness, its practice instructions can be applied to any of the brahma-viharas, including compassion.[125] It points both to the particularities of individuals, and to the view of compassion as an ever-running stream in which all beings, in varying identities and forms, are waves in life's boundless current. This is the current we tap into as we are impacted by vulnerability, giving and receiving compassion as it spills over from the wisdom and courage that evolves in meeting our own pain. Compassion may at times appear distant or blocked, and yet it is an inalienable human capacity. It is our birthright. And it asks that we develop the creativity, flexibility, and trust to meet the barriers and overwhelm that may accompany it.

What does compassionate connection look like? Drawing on Zenju Earthlyn Manuel's image of a circle, we can learn through practice, imagination, and experiment how to sense into this. I ask Esther what has sustained her capacity for compassion during decades working in the National Health Service (NHS):

> The sheer beauty of people and their uniqueness. It doesn't matter who you work with, everybody is so different. I feel privileged that people let me into their lives, allow me to sit with them in pain. Most of the time it does seem that sitting with somebody's suffering, even if they don't get completely better, can in the moment take away that sense of being alone. Some of my most profound experiences have been in the most difficult areas, like working with homeless drinkers or working in an acute ward.

Circles of connection

Many traditions, both religious and secular, honour forebears and ancestors, those on whose shoulders we stand and who have made our lives possible. When my nephew was born, I traced our family tree, discovering my great-great-great-grandmother Janet Fea Fotheringhame Peace, born in Stronsay, Orkney, in 1771, who gave birth to her seventh child on 16 May 1815. As I search the scanned parish records on the *Scotland's People* genealogy website, copperplate handwriting takes shape on my screen. The birth of a daughter to a crofting family on a windswept island of herring and kelp; and a scratched footnote: 'The mother died five hours after the child was born.' What strength was needed to sustain this loss? What happened to the motherless child and her siblings? Someone cared for them. A lineage of care, unrecorded, unsung. Flawed no doubt, and partial, yet making so much possible. Such connections can give depth to a circle of humanity.

Our ancestors need not be genetically related to us. Depending on our identities and social locations, we may be separated from, or rejected by, our birth families. During post-Covid reunions, it was joyful to take a long walk with my 'logical' (rather than biological) family. Pausing in a Peak District field to tell our lockdown stories:

'What happened when your mum fell and broke her femur?'
'How did your daughter cope with student halls in lockdown?'
'What have you learned?'

Countless people have fought for the freedoms we value; a few make it into the history books, and many don't. Harvey Milk, the first openly gay elected official in California, was assassinated in 1978. At the thirtieth anniversary of his death, musician and activist Holly Near addressed the LGBT community, honouring the history and influence of the black civil-rights movement:

> We walk in a long tradition of people who have been wounded and hurt. The rage we felt after these assassinations was so powerful, and we had a choice at that moment to fall prey to grief and rage or to turn those emotions into a movement for social change. There had been precedents before us that to turn those emotions into social change was a much more effective choice, and that's what we did. So along with the sadness and grief comes the excitement that we as human beings have this potential to change the world again and again and again.[126]

Connections to lineage shift the perception of isolation. Two years before same-sex marriage was legalized in England and Wales, while researching LGBT history I found the story of Ann Hants and Henrietta Stokes (passing and living in a male identity as Harry), who were married in Sheffield parish church in 1817.[127] In a similar vein, Out of the Archive musician Val Regan and writer Nicky Hallett celebrate LGBT ancestors, such as Claude Cahun / Lucy Schwob and Marcel Moore / Suzanne Malherbe. Bright young things of the Paris Surrealist scene in the 1920s and 1930s, Cahun and Moore were lovers who made extraordinary art and defied gender norms. During the Nazi occupation of Jersey they hid in plain sight, and embarked on a daring campaign to undermine the occupiers: art as resistance.[128]

Cor, the Latin for 'heart' (giving the French *cœur* and English 'cardiac'), is at the linguistic root of 'courage'. Such stories can strengthen the heart, expand capacity for compassion. However lonely we feel, in the broadest dimension of time and space we are not alone. Whether they are present, absent, alive, or dead, human, non-human, or more-than-human, when we discover and acknowledge these allies they become sources of strength.[129]

As we dwell with existential crises, we may be poignantly aware of our connection to those who will come after us. How can we become good ancestors, rededicating the generosity of those who have come before, and offering what we can for the welfare of the future? Not from guilt or obligation but from a conscious decision to take a place in the circle with humility, aware that out of ignorance we are complicit in actions whose consequences we're unaware of, and that future generations will pay the price for.

During Covid lockdown, I formed a support bubble with a friend and her seven-year-old daughter, cycling to the playground with her on Sundays. One grey autumn afternoon as she sits on a solitary swing, and I, out of habit, gather torn Haribo bags and used wet-wipes to throw in the bin, her voice carries across the tarmac,

'Well done for looking after the planet, I'm proud of you!' and she runs over to give me a high five.

Many young ones aren't afraid to speak out. As I unpack my suitcase on a family visit, my six-year-old niece looks askance,

'Why have you got a plastic comb instead of a wooden one? That's silly!'

Their generation could live into the twenty-second century – there will be profound calls on their resilience.

CREATIVE EXPLORATION

 Guided Meditation – Caring

Invite ancestors and supporters to join you. They may come alone, or in teams, marching bands, or choirs. Imagine them on either side, rooting for you unconditionally. Historical figures known and unknown, friends, singers, artists, activists, neighbours, teachers, animal companions, or the beech trees in the park.

Bring those you are thankful for, and who will remind you when you lose faith.

Write their names, draw them, sing and dance them into community.

Extend this circle of belonging to younger generations, beginning with those who are dear to you, broadening out through images or somatic sensations to the countless ones who will come after. What happens as you sense yourself embedded in a lineage of past, present, and future?

Reconnection

The late 1980s. A Nottingham community centre with formica tables and stackable chairs. A workshop on peace activism titled 'Despair and empowerment in the nuclear age' inspired by an American writer called Joanna Macy. That's all I remember, and all I know about her for years, but I hold her name and the phrase 'Despair and empowerment' close to my heart. These three words illuminate a path to hope, by acknowledging the overwhelm that is second nature to me and partnering it with renewed agency. Joanna Macy's books, and the Work That Reconnects training and community she initiated, are calls to transform despair into creative, collaborative action.[130]

The Scottish philosopher and human ecologist Alastair McIntosh poetically summarizes the path to a middle way between denialism and alarmism:

> Often the question arises: What can we do when we wake up and realise that we've got to do something? One answer is to feed the hungry. Refute the graceless spirit of mere utility. Restore the broken cycles of grace, put right the devastation of the past, and celebrate resurgence of the flows of gratitude, of blessedness, of what gives life.[131]

As we reflect on community support, Esther emphasizes the need to keep reconnecting:

> River: 'It comes back to that sense of connection, and not being alone.'

> Esther: 'Absolutely. If we are this circle that's unbroken, then actually we have quite a lot of power.'

Reconnection builds on the groundwork of pausing, befriending, and enjoying, and extends capacity to find a middle way.

Walking meditation
and the garden becomes
something other than chores left undone –
hawthorn, hoverflies, wood pigeon cooing.
Palate flooded with abundance on this evening
of the hottest day in decades, the balmy air receives
and tremors with the depth of fear, the breadth of mourning:
nothing that can't be held.[132]

What is compassion?

March 2020. We watch Boris Johnson announcing the first lockdown. It seems like a dream, but, as traffic noise stops and the sound of birdsong swells, reality begins to bite. Like millions of others, our community begins to self-organize – street by street, wardens volunteer to bring supplies to those isolating or shielding; local shops organize deliveries for elderly or disabled people; fabrics are recycled to make masks; the casual neighbourly 'How are you?' is freighted with new meaning and sincerity. Covid-19 pushed human vulnerability to the foreground: it was no longer so easy to deny the suffering bound up in our embodiment, or the inevitability and unpredictability of sickness and death.

The pandemic revealed the extraordinary capacity of our species to rise up and care for others. Stories that evidence this were collected initially by KarunaVirus.org, now called Karuna News, whose intent is to amplify the voice of collective compassion by featuring news of everyday people choosing love over fear.[133] Cuba sending a brigade of fifty-two doctors and nurses to Lombardy in Italy at the height of the first deadly wave; a nineteen-year-old from Pune, India, designing a fan to keep doctors in PPE cool after his medic mother arrived home drenched in sweat; a four- and a six-year-old spending their tooth-fairy money on supplies for elderly neighbours in Queensland, Australia.

Covid also exposed the opposites of compassion and generosity: the anxiety that provokes panic-buying; the fear that increases gun sales; the spread of conspiracy theories, often linked to the far right; the pressure to rapidly return to the 'normal' of unsustainable consumption; the hypocrisy of those in public office who consider themselves exempt from the rules they impose on others.

Compassion has become a well-used term in political discourse, on the right as well as the left. After Black Lives Matter uprisings in response to the brutal murder of George Floyd, Donald Trump vowed to control the streets 'with force and compassion'. In May 2022 Boris Johnson promised that the UK government would use 'all their ingenuity and compassion' to support people faced with escalating costs of living, despite charities criticizing the lack of any real action.[134]

Christian Picciolini, a former neo-Nazi, describes how as a bullied teenager he was given acceptance and community by the white supremacy movement. Now committed to helping people leave the far right to connect with humanity and lead compassionate lives, he says, 'The only way to show them that there is nothing to hate, is to show them that there is something to love.'[135]

Angela King, co-founder of Life After Hate, tells how her racist and violent views changed when a woman of colour befriended her in prison, and describes what is needed in working with others from the alt-right:

> She became a friend who treated me like a human being when I didn't feel like a human being. It was simply kind acts from people who knew I was a racist, they knew I was there for a hate crime, and that literally did change the direction of my entire life.
> We have that compassion, share our own experiences, and let people know that there's hope, because there is going to come a day when they rethink what they're doing. It's not about saying the hate and violence are OK, what we're doing is isolating the human from what was done to them and what they did to others.[136]

Being able to see a person as separate from their actions speaks to a radical view of unconditional compassion, and leaves the door open for the possibility of transformation.

CREATIVE EXPLORATION

What does compassion mean to you? What are your associations with the word?

The roots of compassion

The word 'compassion' originates from Latin: *compatior* meaning 'to suffer' (*patior*) 'with' (*com*). In Middle English it meant a literal sharing of affliction or suffering. Just as a musical instrument resonates when another instrument is played nearby, the human body reverberates in response to another's pain. The heart trembles and shakes.

Patior is also the linguistic root of 'patience', the capacity to endure, to calmly bear difficulty. It is akin to humility, to a deeply grounded ability to reflect and learn. In the heat of responding to suffering, our own or others', nearby or far away, patience and humility can be hard to recall. Depending on our conditions and habit patterns we may react by fighting, fleeing, freezing, appeasing, collapsing. Sometimes a superhero persona materializes, we respond by trying to rescue. When we become strongly identified as someone who helps and protects, two other archetypes are strengthened: the victim and the persecutor. When rescuing intensifies and we tremble on the edge of burnout, we may begin to feel victimized ourselves, sometimes by those we are trying to help. The closed loop of the Victim–Persecutor–Rescuer triangle shifts round a notch, but we are still in its grip.[137]

For Esther, the acceptance of her limitations helps mitigate such patterns, as does the support of an embodied practice:

In the early days my Christian faith and sense of God were very strong, a sense that nothing ever rested only at my feet. As I've leaned more into Buddhism it's become an acceptance that I'm all I have, so that's all I can offer. I feel grateful that I was introduced to yoga, because using the body to calm the mind is sometimes more accessible when you are in pain. I can get into a downward-dog pose that takes half the load and creates the space to allow me to sit with the breath.

In the Pali discourses of early Buddhism several words translate as 'compassion'. The most frequent are 'anukampa' (from the verb 'to tremble, shake, reverberate') and 'karuna' (from the root verb *kr*, 'to do or make'). 'Anukampa' occurs around three times more often than 'karuna', and Gil Fronsdal suggests it is a more immediate response of care and caring, rather than the quality developed in meditation.[138] When the Buddha encourages his followers to 'Go forth and practise for the welfare and happiness of all, out of compassion for the world', it is 'anukampa' that is used. In his exploration of compassion in early Buddhism, Analayo writes:

> active expressions of compassion in the early discourses predominantly take the form of teaching the Dharma. ... The term used in such contexts is *anukampa*, which in the early discourses often functions to express compassion in action, whereas *karuna* is the regular choice in contexts related to the meditative practice of compassion.

However, in a footnote he acknowledges that sometimes the reverse is true, citing a sutta where 'the boundless radiation of *metta* leads on to a mental attitude of *anukampa* for all beings.'[139]

Both the external response of compassion in action and the more internal development of compassion as a contemplative practice are active in the sense that they are intentionally cultivated. Whether sitting quietly on a cushion, or reaching out to care for ourselves and others, we are always bringing something into being, planting seeds that may ripen now or later.

Esther picks up on this metaphor:

> Sometimes it's quite difficult to practise compassion equally for oneself and others. I tend to think of it as the garden; if I don't practise regularly, it's like when I don't go into the garden, the weeds are overgrown and it's all over the place. I have to keep on practising or I get pulled into wanting to be perfect, and loving the bits that are shiny and not liking the bits that are dull and tired.

CREATIVE EXPLORATION

If compassion was a place, an activity, a colour, a food, an image, an animal, or a plant, what would it be?

Perils of perfectionism

As Esther highlights, getting pulled into wanting to be perfect is one of the obstacles on compassion's path, where we meet the infinite DIY projects of self-improvement. Nothing is worth doing, we insist, unless I polish up my better qualities, iron out the less appealing features of my personality, sand down my unpleasant habits. We try to construct a life where we are quarantined from inner or outer criticism. Days, weeks, years go by. We think we're getting somewhere but again we become disheartened. There is still so much to dislike and disapprove of in ourselves. In learning to sustain compassion we learn to bear with mistakes, to keep drawing from the well of an infinite and 'wild patience'.[140] We learn to take account of small acts of compassion, rather than dismissing them as irrelevant or pointless in the greater scheme of things.

The compassion thought-police (another version of Mara) are always happy to be on stand-by to compare, rank, and disparage any intentions and acts of compassion. They march up and down tut-tutting, and scribbling notes on a clipboard. Are you doing enough? Should you be more like X or Y? If you were really a good person you would...

And yet, there are ways we can wake up to what needs to change, not through the goading of guilt, but out of care. What happens, for example, when we realize unconscious biases in terms of race, gender, sexuality, class, age, disability, and much more? When someone else points them out? It can be shocking to our self-construct, to the one who longs to be seen as 'a good person'. Is there denial, blaming, collapse, projection? With the support of friendliness and patience towards ourselves as a work-in-progress, we can wake up from delusion, make amends, and gain insight into the causes and conditions that have brought these biases into being, moving from either the comfort zone or the panic zone into the learning and stretch zone. This can be a physical, embodied, and emotional stretching, as much as a cognitive one.

> Allowing something
> to be less than perfect
>   – much less –
> is like a golden thread
> wrapped around the moment,
> a gift for the future.[141]

CREATIVE EXPLORATION

Make a gesture, a mark on the page, a sound. Do it with the intention of being utterly imperfect. What's it like to do this?

Walk by the water[142]

Spring and early summer have brought little rain. In the shallows of the river Derwent, water babbles over ancient stepping-stones. Dippers with brown and white plumage sing from mossy rocks above the placid, peaty currents. I've led creative projects celebrating this body of water that snakes down from the Pennines through the gorges of Derbyshire's Peak District, and on to join the Trent and the North Sea. But I've only recently begun to understand its historical connections to present-day injustice.

 In the eighteenth and early nineteenth centuries the Derwent Valley was a leading site of textile production's industrialization. Inspired by the era of Enlightenment, entrepreneurs like Richard Arkwright and Jedediah Strutt harnessed the Derwent to drive machines and mills that kick-started the Industrial Revolution. They brought agricultural labourers and families, including children, to work in purpose-built factories. Much of the raw cotton processed in these mills was grown and harvested by enslaved African people in the West Indies, Brazil, and the southern states of America.

The greater productivity of the factory system led to unprecedented demands for cotton, the large-scale exploitation of working-class men, women, and children in the industrial cities of northern England, as well as an inhuman, brutal regime of historic global slavery.[143] The cloth was then exported to the British Empire's expanding colonies, fuelling the growth of immense fortunes and inequalities, planting the seeds of extractive capitalism yoked to the myth of eternal economic growth, with a catastrophic legacy for global climate and ecological systems.

In the Slave Compensation Act of 1837, the British government gave £20 million (£17 billion in today's money) in over 46,000 payments to slave owners. This money was invested in the infrastructure and institutions of Victorian Britain. Not a penny, nor any word of apology, was given to those who had been enslaved. 'Racial capitalism' is a term increasingly used by historians to capture these two interrelated systems that continue to dominate the modern world.[144] Kris Manjapra writes: 'legacies of slavery continue to shape life for the descendants of the formerly enslaved, and for everyone who lives in Britain, whatever their origin.'[145]

My steps slow as I recall the privileges inherited from these systems and legacies, including the very freedom to walk with ease along this riverbank. Researching family trees reveals that, like many from Scotland's Highlands and Islands, some of my Orcadian ancestors gained wealth through the trade of enslaved peoples in West Africa, the Americas, and the Caribbean.[146] The writer and activist adrienne maree brown asks: 'What does it mean to honor all our ancestors, including some who colonized, some who share responsibility for creating the mess we humans find ourselves in today?'[147]

Moment by moment there can be a turning towards the fathomless harm caused directly and indirectly to countless people, and to the minds and hearts that have perpetrated these harms. The three fires of greed, hatred, and confusion operate on individual, relational, and societal levels. Can their influence on assumptions, words, and actions be recognized? Can there be a commitment to learn from inevitable mistakes, to decolonize the mind and heart from ignorance? White-body supremacy and racialized identities live in, and distort, the cells and fibres of the heart, mind, body; cultivating compassion unconditionally means to consciously undertake the practice and action of embodied anti-racism, described by Resmaa Menakem as somatic abolitionism.[148]

Rhonda Magee writes:

Transforming identity-based bias and oppression, and dismantling the structures that maintain them, is lifelong work. Its success cannot be measured in the short run, though we may be able to see and feel some positive differences as we go. The long years it has taken to get mired in the problems of racism ensure that it will take many years to get us out. ... It is not merely personal work. It requires that we take a long-term view of what it means to see, to be with, and to correct racist structures for the liberation of all people.[149]

The water continues to flow. The path of the Dharma is said to go against the stream of delusion and reactivity. Step by step across the flood, without forcing and without standing still.

Compassion for oneself

The weight of racial suffering can be heavy on the body, heart, and mind. Most of us want our distress to go away without caring for it. ... Compassion practice serves as an anticoagulant to such burdens. With practice, we experience more inner circulation – more flow, lightness, and openness. ... We begin to realize there is more love in our hearts than anything else – we're just not in the habit of relying on it.

Ruth King[150]

In the *Acrobat Sutta* the Buddha tells the story of two street performers whose art is balancing on bamboo poles. The more experienced acrobat says to their apprentice: 'Come now, climb up the pole and stand on my shoulder. You look after me and I'll look after you.' But the apprentice replies:

> That's not how it is! You must look after yourself and I'll look after myself. That's how, guarding and looking after ourselves, we'll display our skill, collect our fee and get down safely.

The Buddha adds:

> It's just as the apprentice says. Thinking 'I'll look after myself' you should cultivate a foundation of mindfulness. Thinking 'I'll look after others' you should also cultivate a foundation of mindfulness. Looking after yourself you look after others; and looking after others, you look after yourself. How do you look after others by looking after yourself? Through development, cultivation and practice of meditation. And how do you look after yourself by looking after others? Through patience, non-harming, loving-kindness and care.[151]

Compassion for oneself and compassion for others are not separable. Yet self-compassion can feel distant. When we consider it there may be strong cultural or social belief systems that argue against it; there may be a fear of complacency, self-indulgence, or inactivity. But leaving oneself out of compassion's circle is also to concretize and reify the self in a certain way, to adopt, often as a survival strategy, a distorted view of ourselves as unique because of our especially notable *un*worthiness. One of the tenets of Kristin Neff's Self-Compassion Break is to recall one's common humanity, that suffering is part of life, and that all people struggle at times.[152]

Imagine two plants growing next to each other, the same size and shape. Earth, water, light, and air bring the nutrients needed to keep them alive and flourishing. You contemplate these plants, their leaves and flowers shining and blooming. You make a decision. You choose one and begin to neglect it. You cover it over and ignore it. No light or water can enter. This plant is yourself. Why are you less deserving of care? Why would you not treat yourself as equal to any other life form?

CREATIVE EXPLORATION

Scan through your awareness and choose something that feels uncomfortable. Body too cold or hot, a feeling of hunger or thirst, a niggle, an itch, a heaviness, a worry. Notice how your attention can move towards and away from this sensation; the pull to focus on discomfort or push it away. Simply know the difficulty as it is, imagining the space around it. With support of breath and ground, bring a soothing care to yourself, through words, images, or sensations. Linger with any relief that emerges.

Turning towards and witnessing what is hard to bear is a stepping-stone of compassion. This is where we become familiar with tendencies and habits.

Disguises and enemies

Compassion's far enemy is cruelty; the spectrum of opposites includes numbing, disconnection, resentment, disgust, and overwhelm. Pity and saviourism often masquerade as compassion. The word 'opposites' can create an expectation that, if we just get rid of these, a direct route to pure, uncomplicated compassion will open up. But the obstacles are the ingredients we work with, through exploring their layers and effects, and bringing compassion to them too.

Esther's insights about practising with the dimensions of hate and fear enrich our conversations. In Buddhist practice, the stages of cultivating compassion include extending it to difficult people, sometimes described as the enemy. I ask Esther about the obstacles to extending unconditional compassion:

As a black woman I was heavily involved with the Royal College of Nursing and anti-racist movements. If you're anti-something you have to be mindful not to hate, because if you hate then it's difficult to be compassionate. At a Martin Luther King retreat they talked about compassion for your enemy. I had to get my head around feeling compassion for a racist person who wanted to kill me. It's taken a lot of work. In situations where there's hate, you have to stand strong not to hate back. When you hate back, hate is an enemy of compassion.

Esther's wisdom inspires me. The journey of recognizing hate without being caught in it can be a long one, and I often feel like a novice, trying to pause where possible with the physiological signs of hate's presence: trembling, limbs on fire, the abdomen braced and rigid. Can there be compassion for hate and aversion in oneself, the embodied way it flares, tightening and contracting the torso, arms, hands? When there's a strong intention and self-image of being peaceful and loving, it's courageous to acknowledge the seeds of hate, planted by, and germinating because of, particular causes and conditions.

In extending compassion to those we find difficult, there may be situations of harm and abuse where we need to start with slow and careful steps, deeply rooted in compassion for ourselves first and foremost, perhaps imagining that those who wish us harm are a long way away and without the means to hurt us. As Jaya highlighted in Chapter 2, a skilful option is to extend compassion towards the whole situation of harm and hurt. For Esther, a profound belief in the power of love has supported her on the journey to an ever-deepening compassion: 'As well as love, openness is needed, so that when hate shows up people don't just brush it under the carpet.'

One analysis of compassion distinguishes between sympathy, empathy, and service: sympathy as a tacit assumption of superiority, immune to another's troubles; empathy as being in the same boat, able to listen and relate intimately and authentically. A positive image of service envisages taking a place in the orchestra of common humanity, rather than helping, which is not a relationship between equals. With no distinction between those who give and those who receive, compassion becomes a selfless offering rooted in generosity. Echoing this perspective, Norman Fischer cites the meal reflection chanted by Zen practitioners: 'May we with all beings realize the emptiness of the three wheels, giver, receiver, and gift.'[153]

'Service' can have cultural resonances of servitude and a lack of liberty. In British contexts the term 'in service' has historically been applied to domestic workers, often working-class women, vulnerable to abuse and with few rights. If the concept of service can be reclaimed from these connotations, then it can be creatively applied as a reminder that the practice of compassion points towards a non-egoic activity, as something that flows once we get out of the way.

Rachel Naomi Remen, a medical doctor who has lived with chronic illness for forty-five years, writes:

When you help, you see life as weak. When you fix, you see life as broken. When you serve, you see life as whole. Fixing and helping may be the work of the ego, and service the work of the soul. ... From the perspective of service, we are all connected: All suffering is like my suffering and all joy is like my joy. The impulse to serve emerges naturally and inevitably from this way of seeing.[154]

How to discern when a compassionate response is flavoured with pity, helping, rescuing, or controlling? Or by racial, social, and gender-based expectations? Is there such a thing as an authentic compassionate response, rooted in the embodied knowledge that there is no gift, no giver, no receiver? Our motivations for responding to pain and suffering are almost always mixed – the practice of sustaining compassion involves recognizing the many layers as they rise to the surface.

Unravelling

Her confidence has evaporated, social occasions are daunting, and anxiety makes it hard to leave the house. But she is motivated to take a bus into the city once a week to volunteer at a group for women refugees. She is white, privileged by social class, education, and citizenship status. Entering the leaking, draughty community hall she feels shaky, worried that she will have a panic attack or burst into tears. But the external focus of supporting women to learn English, look after the kids, and prepare a meal transforms her mind-state and lifts her spirits.

On the one hand, this could seem like bypassing emotional needs to meet the needs of others; on the other, it could look like a healthy way of switching attention. It could appear to be generosity, and it could look like disempowerment, an undermining of the participants' confidence by volunteers, the majority of whom are white, an unhealthy legacy of dependency. She has an urge to offer practical help in response to the racism and misogyny of the immigration system, as well as a need to connect and find respite from mental turmoil. There is a white-saviour fantasy, a focus on other people's problems that puts her own in perspective, the distraction of practical tasks, a latent sense of comfort and superiority that boosts her self-esteem. There are the wide disparities in privilege, power, and opportunity. There is also joy, warmth, and generosity, the delight of connecting as a community that has met in this way for many years and through many challenges. There is the constant moving and balancing of harm and non-harm, present and potential, that lies at the centre of complex, condition-dependent lives.

Some of these things become clear in the moment, and some clarify over time. Only in seeing them honestly is it possible to change attitudes and actions. In the lifetime process of orienting towards compassion, can we find the humility to keep learning?

CREATIVE EXPLORATION

What are your fantasies of an ideal compassionate being?

How can you tell when compassion is flavoured with pity, helping, fixing, or rescuing?

Response

Compassion is sometimes described as the love that responds, that turns towards difficulty or suffering and listens deeply, witnesses, acts. A response that is as natural and unforced as when we reach half-awake to adjust a pillow under our heads. Active listening as a compassionate response – represented by the image of Kwanyin, the one who listens – is often underestimated. Pausing and listening help to clarify intention, soften reactivity, give space for steadier action.

When I ask Esther to define compassion, she speaks about how being part of the human community informs her practice, and how she is also influenced by psychotherapy, Buddhism, and Christianity:

I suppose the Matthieu Ricard view of compassion as not just recognizing suffering, or recognizing being human, but also the intention to do something and being activated to ease the suffering. Just as the Good Samaritan went out of his way to be kind to someone from a different denomination. It's not just sympathy, that feeling for someone, but that desire to alleviate their suffering.

CREATIVE EXPLORATION

Gently, and with the support of breath and contact with ground, bring to mind a place where there is suffering and hardship. This could be in your location, somewhere nearby, or further away. Feel into the capacity of the listening heart to know this as suffering, to bear witness, and to wish for soothing and healing. Gently and patiently notice any impulses to turn away, or to reach towards it. Stay with the listening, witnessing, and caring for a while longer. Take as much time as you need.

The Buddha's backache

When I first heard this story and sought it out in the Pali suttas, I was moved by the compassionate action the Buddha takes to ease his pain.[155] I tried to convey some of that human response in this poem, finding it easier to relate to an ageing body with backache than a superhuman persona with metaphysical powers. Gotama is the clan name for the historical figure we know as the Buddha. Ananda was his cousin, close companion, and attendant for the last twenty-five years of his life.

Getting on in years, Gotama addressed
the gathered crowds,
a moon between the trees,

but then he paused and turned to Ananda,
'You teach tonight, my friend,
this backache troubles me'.

What do I know of Dipa Ma,
Julian of Norwich,
Jesus, Gandhi,

but weren't they too the clay grown tall,
with pulses that trembled and stilled,
feet that grew sore,

blisters, cancers, ulcers,
our human tragedies,
I writing this, you with your eyes and ears.

Perhaps the body's book was their companion
opened on pages bare words
falter to translate;

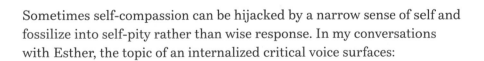

how can the measureless be reached
without long journeys
where blood pounds, bones shake?

I recollect the Buddha lying in the dark
easing his back as I soothe mine
with careful hands, the language of the heart.

Sometimes self-compassion can be hijacked by a narrow sense of self and
fossilize into self-pity rather than wise response. In my conversations
with Esther, the topic of an internalized critical voice surfaces:

I know when I'm being compassionate because I talk to myself the way I talk to my children. I know when compassion is lacking because there's that harsh voice:

'What's wrong with you Esther, come on!'

When compassion is there, I'm more likely to see my pain, and to see that not reaching the standard I'd set myself doesn't need criticism, it needs love.

When I note that we keep coming back to the word 'love' despite its complicated connotations, Esther responds:

Love is tangible. From a practitioner point of view it's important that we don't become clinging with it. When I'm clingy I'm more likely to have jealousy or resentment, and when I'm being simply loving there's an acceptance of the flawed me.

I return to the image of the Buddha and his backache, a loving touch that responds in the moment, without clinging, catastrophizing, or denying. Simple, and not always easy.

The supple heart

What is meant when speaking about the heart in the context of compassion? Both 'heart' and 'mind' are used to translate *citta*. Of the three main words for 'mind' in Pali, 'citta' is most widely used and carries the most varied meanings. It can be roughly interpreted as 'mindset' or 'mental processes' with an emphasis on the emotive side of mind. Ajahn Sucitto defines 'citta' as 'that which is impacted and that which responds'. It is also said to be that which is liberated.

Heartbreak seems at times an entirely appropriate response to loss and pain, and to the immeasurable depths of harm in our world, but relentless impact without malleability leads to fracturing. Years ago on a meditation retreat I couldn't stop crying. I wandered through the corridors and gardens, flooded with grief, unable to reconcile myself to systemic violence. In a group meeting with a teacher, I sat silently, tears pouring down my cheeks. After everyone else had spoken she turned to me. I muttered something about overwhelm.

'You can swim in the sea of suffering forever', she said.

Her tone of voice was gentle, but her words shook me out of the painful mind-state, as if a bucket of water had been emptied over my head. I didn't fully understand what she meant, but my body responded. There was a physical sense that I'd been given ground to stand on, a choice, a chance to stand beside suffering and see it for what it was without being its prisoner. Later I could recognize that part of my grief was an inability to accept powerlessness, the pain of an ego eternally hammering its fists on the locked door of injustice, disconnected from the simple realities of being just one voice in a choir, one instrument in the band.

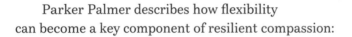

Parker Palmer describes how flexibility can become a key component of resilient compassion:

> Every day exercise your heart by taking in life's little pains and joys. That kind of exercise will make your heart supple, the way a runner makes a muscle supple, so that when it breaks (and it surely will) it will break not into a fragment grenade, but into a greater capacity for love.[156]

This image of a supple heart can support the courage to respond with tenderness to life, allowing us to be unafraid to let tears or laughter come when they need to. Unafraid to respond as best we can to all that we meet.

Esther and I discuss the appeal of a heart that can stretch to accommodate joys and sorrows, so it doesn't shatter into a million pieces when the inevitable heartbreak arrives. The years that she has spent on hospital wards come to mind, as Esther muses:

> It's a lovely analogy because a healthy heart is exercised and supple, whereas when it is hardened and unyielding it becomes diseased. So maybe that's how we work on compassion, work on softening...

The world outside the confines of our skin, the world we sometimes call nature (though we are part of nature), supports the compassionate heart to soften into something greater than 'just me'. Like many, I find consolation in nature, as I write this taking a moment to look out at the silver-birch trees beyond the window, the shape and movement of their dancing leaves, memories of walking in their shade and leaning against their trunks. In Chapter 2 Jaya describes the gifts of the natural world, and Esther also gains strength from the earth's unconditional support:

> I have been very lucky to enjoy running
> and walking. There's something
> about nature, whether it's a
> river or a tree or a mountain,
> that reminds you that you
> are only a tiny little bit of this
> beautiful world around us.
> When you sit by the seaside and
> look at the waves and think of what
> they've witnessed, it puts everything
> into perspective and makes you
> very humbled. The feeling of the
> feet on the ground reminds me:
> This Mother never turns me away,
> when I'm bad she always welcomes me.

CREATIVE EXPLORATION

Go outside. If you can't go outside, look through a window.
Let a part of nature come into your awareness and dwell with it for a few minutes, taking in shape, colour, texture, light, sound, smell. Soften into your breathing and recall that this being is breathing too, whether through photosynthesis, gills, skin, or lungs. Recollect that the earth, the sun, the air are supporting you and this other life, as well as all life forms in this moment. Can you soften through your body, mind, and heart into that support?

Fierce compassion

As a junior doctor, Lucy Chan saved a patient's life by trusting her instinct that something was wrong and contradicting the opinion of a senior consultant. She reflects:

> The amount of suffering in the world makes my heart break again and again, but every time I stand up, speak out, support those in need, I feel a strength there, a strength that stems from pure love, a love that encompasses courage and wisdom, a love that is powerful. That is fierce compassion.[157]

Compassion is not passive in the face of what is harmful. Compassion can mean saying 'No', and not remaining silent. Esther gives a moving example of standing up for her values, and the consequences of doing this:

> When the gay marriage law was being passed there was a lot of hate expressed in our church, and our family confronted it. We stormed out of Mass at different times, and we ended up losing a church community, but we knew we stood for love.

In practising fierce compassion, we also discover where we haven't stood up for ourselves and where we need to safeguard our energies and capacities. Through research with people who are compassionate by vocation, such as spiritual teachers, clergy, monks, and nuns, the self-help author and social psychologist Brené Brown found that many had 'boundaries of steel'. Setting limits about what is, and is not, OK protected them from resentment. Boundaries can denote respect rather than division; compassion minus boundaries is not genuine, let alone sustainable.[158] Being clear about having limited capacities while remaining open-hearted and generous is a great aspiration, and it takes patience to learn from the times when we over-reach. Often it is essential to protect what we say 'Yes' to, by saying 'No' to other demands on our time and attention. Practice

and honesty help us to discern more clearly where habits of self-sacrifice might be operating. These patterns are often linked to *vibhava tanha*, a form of tanha or unquenchable thirst that underpins suffering, manifesting in craving for non-being and self-denial, an aversion to ourselves, our motivations, and desires.

As my conversation with Esther draws to a close, she returns to the importance of community:

> In the field of social justice there are often thoughts like: 'Am I doing it right?' or 'How much do you do?' Injustice is the opposite of compassion, and yet we live in such an unjust world.
>
> I see this young man sitting outside the Sainsbury's near my work,
>
> 'Can I buy you a sandwich?'
>
> 'I've eaten already but could you buy me some cigarettes? Otherwise I'm going to be picking up dog-ends from the road.'
>
> And I realize that a packet of cigarettes costs £16...
>
> How do we negotiate a world that's so unfair and be true to our values and able to survive without bankrupting ourselves? It's a practice, leaning more into values and being clear what the values are. That's where being part of a community of practitioners becomes powerful. Alone I can't feed even half the people in Hackney, but as a community we can bring change, we can influence. When we look at legislation over the last few decades, we see how much change has been made. Recently I went to a gay wedding. Everybody showed up, and celebrated, there was no 'tolerating', this was full celebration. We can change things but it's going to take time, and whatever action we make as a community needs to be in keeping with our values, embodying the cultivation of the wholesome.

CREATIVE EXPLORATION

Think of something or someone who blocks or undermines your capacity to care. Practise saying 'No' or setting boundaries (with yourself and/or others). What happens?

Heart's release

In stretching and challenging our assumptions and perceptions, we can craft ourselves (and will inevitably be crafted over time) into better companions to ourselves and others, more skilful instruments of service and care rooted in interconnectedness. Traditional images of meditative compassion point to its liberating potential for the heart and mind's release. What do they release into? The twin supports of embodiment and imagination can assist in finding metaphors: a voice enmeshed in a greater sound, an instrument in an ensemble, or one fragment of a vast network.

The Pali suttas give a simile for compassion (as well as metta, joy, and equanimity) radiating over the entire world like a conch-blower, whose notes are heard far and wide, 'abundant, expansive, limitless, free of enmity and ill will'.[159] A memory comes of strolling through a ruined medieval church in the Portuguese city of Coimbra, and being suddenly shaken by the resounding notes of an unseen saxophonist, jazz repertoire seamlessly bridging the centuries, reverberating on the golden stone and thickening the air.

When we take a seat at the brahma-viharas' hearths or touch into their unconditional magnitude, whether in meditation or through the relationship we consciously undertake with the world, sometimes the external beneficial effects are immediate, but often they're unknown and intangible. However, even when nothing external seems to change, *we* are changed. Often not in ways we expect, nor in the timescales we'd like. But tangible in the smallest of acts such as instinctively moving an insect to safety, as well as in profound moments, witnessing a birth or being present while a loved one takes their last breath.

In the characteristically repetitious style of the Pali suttas, a meditator is encouraged to sustain the radiating sound of compassion, grounded in harmlessness, blowing their horn, and making themselves heard in all directions, developing the heart's release. Reminders of the different mediums in which compassion can be expressed, inwardly, outwardly, in meditation, and in action, are shown through different verbs, as if emphasizing the infinite dimensions in which the brahma-viharas can be practised:

cultivated, brought into being
    developed and practised
        made a vehicle and a basis
            kept up
                consolidated
                    properly implemented[160]

CREATIVE EXPLORATION

Take a walk outside, or if you can't go outside move away from the page or screen. Stretch your body and take a few conscious breaths. As you move or walk, experiment with opening your awareness towards caring. Perhaps the care for yourself in taking a break. Perhaps care for the people you pass, or the care that you see in something you encounter, or care for any pain or sorrow nearby or further away. Consciously engage with the ever-present flow and field of giving and receiving compassion, including through a felt bodily sense, and explore how this field can expand.

Chapter 5
LETTING BE

What shall remain as my legacy?
The spring flowers,
the cuckoo in summer,
the autumn leaves.

Ryokan[161]

Fluidity

The cosmos is infinitely complex, there are countless perspectives that can't be conceived. Easier to grasp if considering distant galaxies, but also true of the universe of relationships and social locations. If we investigate our habitual ways of looking, we can begin to see an engrained tendency to lock onto one perception, and view everything through that filter or lens. The ability to pause, step back, and creatively invoke other perspectives blossoms alongside greater capacity for equanimity or steadiness.

There is always more to our perception of ourselves and others than we think. Outdated images and stories block and hinder, often without us realizing, and mean that we can't grow or adapt. We bind others in the same way, by imagining or assuming that we know who they are. What we call 'selves' are made of many things that are not ours: the names we were given, the language we speak, the trillions of bacteria in our gut microbiome, the bodies of knowledge we've inherited, the atoms of oxygen, carbon, hydrogen, borrowed from plants, animals, minerals, and recycled when we die, transforming back into the spring flowers, summer cuckoo, autumn leaves. These components are in perpetual flux; there is no single, unchanging, permanent essence that can be pinned down as 'me' or 'mine'. This 'emptiness' of fixity can also be understood conversely as 'fullness', the infinite possibility and liberation that unfolds when the doors of perception are open. This liberating way of perceiving *anatta* – not-self or emptiness – is a radical and unique strand of the Buddha's teaching, and a deep support for sustaining compassion.

Perceiving anatta is not an end point, but indicates towards a path that endlessly unfolds. By shaking us out of fixity, like a snake shedding the skin it has outgrown, it frees up the tendency to get bogged down in the burning dilemmas of our lives: what shall I do? How can I live well? How will I care for what I love and for that which calls me? Vital questions that enliven and enrapture or mire the questioner in regret, guilt, and burnout.

Alongside this are the realities of conditioned and intersecting identities, and these too can be doorways to freedom. Larry Yang writes:

> The beauty of the Dharma is that everything – *everything*, even all the particulars of identity – is integral to our spiritual practice. Accordingly, freedom is not just about transcending identity but embracing it until what is beyond the experience of identity reveals itself.[162]

A musician in an orchestra must lose their individuality to some extent, be both distinct from and immersed in the soundscape, hearing their own notes clearly enough to know they ring true, but aiming to blend them with those of other players. In this way the art of sustaining compassion invites us to take ourselves more lightly. Yes, there is somebody here, playing the instrument of their being as best they can, discordant or harmonious, letting the sound travel out in all directions. And there is an infinite array of other musicians, with instruments and skills beyond anyone's wildest dreams. Dependently arising with each other and with unknowable aeons of conditions. At times one player or section of melody comes to the foreground, but always falls away again, back into a coursing, rolling stream. In moments there is simply the sense of letting the music play through you.

David W. Robinson-Morris, writing in *Lion's Roar*, alongside Buddhist teachers of African descent, describes the African philosophy of *ubuntu*:

> Ubuntu is a deep and embodied understanding that human beings are not born but formed in community and relationship with one another. ... Perhaps, it was ubuntu that allowed the dispersed and enslaved Africans – my ancestors – to survive the brutality of slavery and the loss of their homelands, mother tongues, and customs, while never questioning their humanity. All human life began on the continent of Mother Africa, so we – the people of the African diaspora – are the people of humanity's birth. Understanding this confers upon us an embodied dignity in the face of the white supremacist ideology, which has run rampant over the globe. Our humanity can never be questioned. ...

Similar to ubuntu is the Buddhist concept of interbeing or interdependent co-arising – the understanding that nothing is separate, self-reliant, or self-contained. All phenomena arise within and from a network of mutuality, an ecosystem of being.

There is no division between human and human, or human and nature, or human and spirit; all things are moving away from fragmentation to wholeness (or complete emptiness). Both ubuntu and Buddhist interdependence are generous ontologies that provoke an awareness of the interwovenness of this web called life and what it means to be a human being in relationship with all sentient beings.[163]

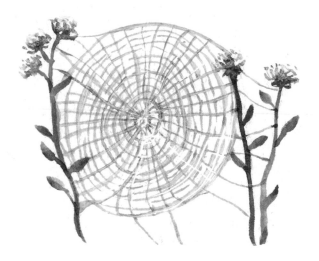

In seeking to understand more fully the nature of emptiness, interdependence, and equanimity, I turned to Yanai Postelnik, whose teaching and guidance I've valued for many years. Yanai, who is of European and Asian ethnicity, grew up in New Zealand and has taught meditation and Buddhist practice internationally for thirty years. Inspired by the Thai Forest Tradition and the transformative power of the natural world, he has devoted significant time to activism and non-violent civil disobedience, calling for an appropriate response by government to the climate, ecological, and social-justice emergencies.

Here he reflects on the wisdom that underpins this brahma-vihara:

Things are not in our control and are not always the way we want them to be. There's a fluidity to how they arise that points to the way they are not owned by us. We can describe this as anatta, that there is no fixed or separate owner to the experience, which is not to say that there isn't a flow of life we can refer to and understand usefully. Connection and relationship to what is around us, the ground from which we arise, are the basis for returning to what we care about, without it becoming something that weighs upon 'just me'. Disconnection and overwhelm happen when we live within an inner world that feels separate, or from a place where we don't remember that 'It's not *just* me, it's not *just* mine.' This points to a shared co-participation in life, rather than (in the classic Buddhist phrases) 'It's not me, not mine.' Seeing that what we are is neither fixed nor separate from what we are amidst makes it clear that the concerns we recognize in our world must be part of our own practice.

CREATIVE EXPLORATION

What image, practice, or philosophy from your heritage and culture expresses the interwovenness of life?

Lightness

Sustaining compassion may feel a weighty enterprise, yet it challenges us to take ourselves and our aspirations lightly as well as seriously. Just as the out-breath supports grounding, so the in-breath allows expansion. Feel and imagine the in-breath as it fills and moves your ribcage, spine, back, limbs. Our lungs and hearts take in and metabolize the oxygen excreted by plants, trees, and phytoplankton; we grow a little into the space around us. With the next in-breath, enjoy the sensation of the body lightening a little, a slight lift, as if on the crest of a wave.

Who we think we are and believe ourselves to be can become a fixed knot, a done deal, even a prison. We encounter this most strongly when pain strikes, when a loved one leaves or dies, when things are not what we want or expect, when we meet dissatisfaction, imperfection, or injustice. Taking ourselves lightly enables uncoupling from views that cement the train tracks of habitual thought patterns and the rumbling, ancient carriages that run on them: 'It *shouldn't* be like this. I *should* be like that. They're *always* like this. It's *never* going to be like that.'

Lightness is not weightlessness; our souls and bodies require the tender blessing of gravity, the nourishment of healthy attachment, physical and psychological. But, amidst urgency, taking ourselves lightly whilst cleaving to intentions of harmlessness and care can be revolutionary.

An understanding of the impermanent, constantly changing flow of life supports insight into the inherent emptiness of self, and of all experience. This is not a channel for denial or nihilism. There is something and someone here, it's just not what we think it is. Rob Burbea writes:

> What matters is the freedom and love that comes from realization of the emptiness of all phenomena. ... When there is insight, we know that how and what we see are not simply givens, but are the colourable and malleable, magical, material of empty appearances.[164]

CREATIVE EXPLORATION

Remember or imagine a time of feeling connected to, and an inalienable part of, something much larger and at the same time profoundly unknowable or mysterious, like a wave rising and subsiding in an ocean. What feels enjoyable, interesting, even exciting about this?

Leaping

My first conscious encounter with someone who took themselves lightly was in April 1988 at Westminster Central Hall, London. I was twenty-four. A friend suggested we go to hear the Dalai Lama speak. I was curious about meditation but knew little about it. My mum was ill with terminal cancer, and life was in turmoil. Perching on slippery wooden seats in the upper circle of the huge hall, we stared at the person on stage who confounded any preconceptions of how a Buddhist monk might behave. Humour and integrity wove around each other in a compelling combination. His eyes twinkled as he giggled, and his face creased into smiles. A personification of ease and lightness. Only much later did I begin to grasp the depth of his personal suffering, and the suffering of the Tibetan people.

Recalling this encounter, another memory surfaces; the location is the street outside the same hall, more than thirty years later. Hundreds of climate protestors are milling about; some lie on the tarmac locked on to each other through sturdy tubes. There are tents, food vans, banners, drummers, singers. At the same time, police move through the crowds, seizing possessions and making arrests. Tension ramps up, anxiety is tangible. Suddenly those around me exclaim and start looking down the street past the entrance of Central Hall. I make out some large, bounding figures, heading this way. I freeze. Is this a police tactic? Are we going to be flattened? More of the creatures come into view. A herd of kangaroos ten feet tall bouncing vigorously but carefully between protestors. My heart leaps. This may not be a burning bush or an angel, but it sure feels like a miracle. The kangaroos – Aussies in brown fur costumes with long tails and pouches – jump happily between us. They carry a sign: Roo-bellion. We make way, applaud, hoot with laughter. The tension defuses.[165]

CREATIVE EXPLORATION

What helps shift you into more lightness of being? What form does this lightness take?

Not knowing

It is a paradox that acknowledging just how much we don't know leads to more wisdom, indeed is sometimes said to be the definition of wisdom.[166] Knowledge is often confused with wisdom. I open the news app on my phone and surf from one compelling headline to the next, caught in the net of believing that the more I know, the greater clarity I'll have about how to be and what to do. After a few minutes, despondent and overwhelmed, I scroll off to find a new recipe or to see if my latest post has been liked. Not knowing means giving up the myth that I am in control, the belief that, if I just try hard enough, get everything lined up, I can finally let go and be at peace.

> warm evening
> almost full moon
> honeysuckle
> stippled sky
> dark-green shadows
> I keep it all
> at arm's length
> so as not to become
> a walking tree
> a cloud fading[167]

We tend to revolve around one form of apparent certainty placed at the centre of our lives, and yet there is a beauty in questioning and shifting that compulsion. A passage in the *Atthakavagga* describes the danger of holding tenaciously on to fixed views:

Entrenched in truths of their own,
They call 'good' whatever they depend on.

Lusting for debates and plunging into assemblies,
They take each other to be fools.
They speak relying on what others have said.
Passionate for praise, they call [themselves] skillful.[168]

Staying open to the creative, empowering edges of not knowing does not equate with *avijja* – confusion or ignorance, a disconnection from impermanence and vulnerability. There is the intention to move forward, act, plant seeds, not knowing if or how they will germinate, motivated not by a hankering for predictable results, but relinquishing the self that seeks to be validated and in charge. I bow to the hunger to be The One Who Knows. Remembering the possibility of tenderness and metta, an image comes of moving through infinite acres of muslin curtains that cloud the onward journey and must be gently eased aside again and again.

Yanai expands on this aspect of meeting life's vicissitudes:

Equanimity is not about being untouched or unaffected by the world. It's often described in relation to the worldly winds: pleasure and pain, gain and loss, success and failure, good or poor reputation. These tend to define our sense of who we are: am I OK? Am I lovable? Am I acceptable? There's the simple level of things we find pleasurable or difficult, and then there's the deeper investment we have in experiences we wish to reflect a certain sense of 'me'. We want to be regarded positively, and that has a place, but if it becomes something that unconsciously drives our behaviour then that's problematic and limiting.

CREATIVE EXPLORATION

What are you hanging on to? What outcome can be let go of in this moment?

Steadying each other

When we look deeply into experience, it becomes clear how little control we have. There is no intention of harbouring an irritation or becoming distracted, and yet here we are again. But we are not completely at the mercy of life's tides; we can have influence.

Although the interpersonal aspects of the other brahma-viharas are easily identifiable – metta and compassion for others, or appreciative joy in another's happiness – equanimity as an actively relational path can seem less obvious. To simply wish for another's balance and send a steadying nod in their direction feels somewhat detached, and falls short of the qualities symbolized by the tree's shade and protection in Longchenpa's poem.

Perhaps relational equanimity is more helpfully conveyed through action and presence. Thich Nhat Hanh describes the suffering of people escaping Vietnam in small boats. More than a million refugees left Vietnam in this way between 1975 and 1995; between 200,000 and 400,000 did not survive.

> Often the boats are caught in rough seas or storms, the people may panic, and boats can sink. But if even one person aboard can remain calm, lucid, knowing what to do and what not to do, he or she can help the boat survive. His or her expression – face, voice – communicates clarity and calmness, and people have trust in that person… One such person can save the lives of many.[169]

Ajahn Sucitto recalls a moment of intense composure during the ordeal of being robbed while on pilgrimage in north-east India:

> They all had axes and staves. The leader glared at me through twisted features and raised his axe.
>
> Funny how your mind goes clear when the options disappear. Why struggle against the inevitable? The only freedom was to go without fear. I bowed my head and pointed the top of my skull toward him, drew the blade of my hand along it from the crown of my head to the brow. 'Hit it right there.' Something shifted; he backed off, waving his axe and

muttering angrily. I stepped forward and repeated the action. Give it away; let it all go.

Things settled. He lowered his axe.[170]

Staying steady can dramatically alter the course of events and have a profound effect on others.

Another image for equanimity: the training wheels or stabilizers fixed to a bicycle when we are learning to ride. We may need to keep reattaching them to remember what steadies and realigns us. Before training wheels, toddlers learn on balance bikes with no pedals, kept steady by the child's feet. Little by little the sensations of balancing are absorbed and grow into the ability to ride, but only through the confidence and trust given in those early stages when you can touch the ground and prevent yourself from falling.

Yanai describes how equanimity is not about fixity:

It's important to have equanimity with one's lack of equanimity, and to have compassion for it. Balance is not a fixed point, it's something that's found by being off balance, coming into balance then getting off balance the other way. At the heart of the Buddha's teaching is the balance between two extremes: one where we lean into the knowledge that what's happening is profoundly tragic and probably beyond avoiding. And leaning also into the other side: that the nature of life is that it's not forever, that the beautiful and distressing are woven together, so many blessed movements of learning, growing, of human potential being honoured and supported in places where it's not been, more than any of us can conceive of or understand.

As the thread of kalyana-mittata and community comes to the foreground again, Yanai reflects that equanimity is never a solitary endeavour:

It's rare that a human being can stay in balance by themselves. Understanding our interdependence points to the need to keep reaching out for support. The pull towards either disengaging or feeling overwhelmed is counterbalanced by a willingness and commitment to keep connecting with others, whether that is the process of our inner life, or the patterns playing out in the world. The heart finds release, relief, and equanimity through connectedness itself, separate from one's degree of success or non-success.

CREATIVE EXPLORATION

Who or what are your training wheels?

What helps you to move evenly on uneven ground?

Emergency. Agency

Torrential rain batters the ground as I return from a morning run. Later the sun blazes and thunder clouds gather in the west, the tail end of a tropical cyclone. Weather in this corner of north-western Europe is increasingly unpredictable and violent. Last winter the river surged and burst its banks after days of record rainfall. Houses were abandoned to floodwater; some are still uninhabitable. Further down the valley, a woman was swept to her death by flash floods. In Mozambique thousands of acres lie under water, hundreds of people have been killed, hundreds of thousands displaced. From the Arctic to California to Australia, fires are burning.

'Our house is on fire', warns Greta Thunberg, whose solo school strike in August 2018 kick-started Fridays for Future, the youth-led climate-strike movement. If our houses were on fire, would we carry on as if nothing was happening? How do we live with the climate emergency and the intersecting emergencies of social and racial injustice, taking action as best we can but without ricocheting between panic and denial?

Take a breath. Feel your feet on the floor, the places where your body rests back and downwards towards the earth. Tune in

to the currents passing through awareness. Can you turn towards the responses in your mind and body with tenderness? In this way compassion leads towards steadiness, agency, and empowerment.

When I first heard the word 'equanimity' it seemed both attractive and alien. I gazed at calm images of the Buddha with hostility and envy. Hostility because they seemed to sum up a tradition that privileged male embodiment, and an approach that felt detached and intellectual. Envy because I longed for some peace and respite from the extremes of either hypervigilance or collapse. Could there be a place for passionate engagement, for rage and heartbreak as well as steadiness on this path?

'Equanimity' was the word that the nineteenth-century translators of the Pali canon reached for to convey 'upekkha'. Unlike English translations for the other brahma-viharas, 'equanimity' is not an everyday word; if someone were to ask, 'How are you?', 'Equanimous' would be a strange and antiquated response. As other translations for 'upekkha', the Pali–English dictionary lists 'disinterest, unaffectedness, lack of involvement or reaction, neutrality'. None of these speaks to the predicament of a short human life caught in the multiple intersecting crises of late capitalism. None feels congruent with a creative path that calls for a commitment to human flourishing and makes room for spontaneity, vulnerability, and error.

The etymology of 'upekkha' suggests 'looking over'. I picture someone surveying a plain from a hilltop, able to see all angles. Can looking over be prevented from degenerating into overlooking?

For its effectiveness, equanimity relies on its brahma-vihara companions. Kindness protects equanimity from being cold. Compassion prevents equanimity from becoming detached. Joy lightens the equanimous heart so that it doesn't take itself too seriously.

I ask Yanai how he defines equanimity:

> Sometimes it seems oppositional: 'You can't be equanimous about what is of deep concern in the world and in our society!' The way I understand it is primarily the ability to be impacted without being pushed into reactivity. To be touched by life, but not to have one's response driven by greed, hatred, and delusion. It's important to distinguish it from indifference to what is harmful or unwholesome. There's a clear recognition in the Buddha's teaching of the qualities, behaviours, and ways of engaging that lead towards wellbeing for oneself, others, and the world, and those which lead towards greater distress, disharmony, and that which is hard to bear.

To remember and return to steadiness does not mean being a magnet with a force field pushing all things an equal distance away. Dare we aspire to be close up and steady, or at least tracking the movement from steadiness to unsteadiness, drawing on the support of pausing, slowing, taking one moment at a time?

CREATIVE EXPLORATION

What does equanimity mean to you?

What are your associations with balance and steadiness?

Balancing

A statue of the Buddha, Kwanyin, or another representation of equanimity can give the impression that the material – stone, wood, metal – is the thing to emulate. The softness and vulnerability of human flesh is not evident. For several hundred years after he died, there were no statues of the Buddha, only aniconic images of footprints, or the wheel or stupa that symbolized the teachings.[171] After Alexander the Great's conquests and the influence of Hellenic art that spread in their wake, statues of the Buddha seated in meditation started to appear through the Indian subcontinent. These statues were in the image of Greeks and Persians with lighter skin and Roman noses, denying Gotama's ancestry as a brown or black person born in the foothills of the Himalayas on the Indian subcontinent. Images can call forth deep aspirations, and they can also obscure the truth. If equanimity is reframed as balance or steadiness, its embodied nature comes to the fore. Picture a tightrope walker or a yoga practitioner in tree pose : it's clear that balance is never fixed because a living body is always in motion. Even when we are still, there are micro-moments of movement. Balance is in relation to the ground, the force of gravity, movement of breath, the body's pulsing. Equanimity as balance is not fixity in relation to compassion, the natural impulse of the heart to alleviate pain. Equanimity is an inclusive perspective that sees sorrow at the same time as it knows the ending of sorrow, that remembers joy in the same moment that it knows pain.

Tchiyiwe Chihana balances working in a systems-change organization in South Yorkshire with hosting television and radio shows for African Voices Platform, the media company she owns, and supporting arts and culture activities led primarily by black women. I ask her how she finds and regains balance:

Because most of my work addresses complex situations, navigating to find solutions and informing policy, my creative life is a deliberate effort to find something different from trying to solve the world's crises. So I enjoy spending time with Utopia Theatre and Roots Mbili Theatre, not as a frontline creative but supporting the production process, reading scripts, being in the rehearsal room, giving input. It's where I'm most at peace, most calm; it is work, but work that centres me. With African Voices Platform I create spaces for people who are doing big things, good things, lovely things, but because they're from the African community, or from people-of-colour communities, they won't be seen in mainstream media. That again is work, yes, but there's a fulfilment there that I'm doing something practical to see the world change.

The public impact, that's where the burnout comes in for me. A few years ago, I realized that, much as I love these things, it means I'm also occupying space that somebody else could be taking up. I was being counterproductive to my aims of seeing more people being visible. Taking a back seat gave me time to rechannel, reposition, and I've been using that to find balance. I'm very deliberate about what I can take and cannot take. And sometimes I disappear, I sit and read and watch what others are doing from a distance. I literally disappear, I'm not available, but I'm enjoying what others are producing.[172]

I ask Yanai for images from his practice and understanding:

The image I often turn to is the keel of a ship that protrudes down into deeper water, and keeps the boat upright so the wind, waves, and current don't capsize it. Having a connection to something that runs deeper in our hearts and psyches than just the circumstances of our experience. Sometimes these will be more fortunate and favourable, and sometimes less so. We learn to have equanimity with these, to find a capacity to see them and not become identified with them.

The keel's vertical quality reflects a connection with something greater, with life in its myriad forms, expressions, and vastness, a sense of a deeper ground. In Buddhist terms it could be expressed as our awakened nature. This gives us a way to orient that stabilizes

the ship of our heart-mind, even when it is subject to wind, wave, storm, and even shipwreck.

Other images include the element of earth, solid and substantial. Or a tree trunk that remains flexible; though the leaves might be blown off, it stays rooted. Or a mountain that's unmoved by the weather passing over it, and yet may feel every drop of rain, every snowflake and gust of wind.

CREATIVE EXPLORATION

What images from your experience or imagination remind you of your capacity to regain balance?

Where can you find steadiness in this moment?

Untangling

In the journey of supporting and keeping compassion alive, the heart will tremble and break open. We may come from a culture where the emotion, physical sound, and sight of heartbreak are unsupported or prohibited. Mara in their form as the inner critic may tell us that heartbreak is failure. The compassion thought-police may tell us that we lack enough steadiness or joy. That we lack maturity.

When we begin to take in and understand the extent of historical, present-day, and future suffering, the apparently unending expressions of human cruelty, heartbreak can seem the only appropriate response. If we develop a supple heart, responsive but light, it can break into solace, into tenderness for ourselves and others.

The etymology of the Pali word 'dukkha' suggests a badly fitting, misaligned wheel on a cart's axle, resulting in an uncomfortable, bruising ride where the passengers are thrown about. 'Dukkha' is often translated as 'suffering' but can be rendered as the full spectrum of dissatisfaction, discontent, vulnerability, and stress. The Buddhist path of practice identifies three key obstructions, fires, or poisons as the springboard for dukkha. Fear is not specified in this list, but it's a birthplace for all of them:

- I'm afraid of loss or instability so I acquire more and can't give up what I have. If I could only get more, materially or spiritually, then I would feel content... I'm in the grip of greed.
- I'm afraid that circumstances or people I don't know or understand will impact me, or threaten my livelihood, my home, my children's future... My heart becomes ruled by aversion and hatred.
- I'm afraid that any decision I make will be the wrong one; I don't know whose advice to listen to; I doubt myself and others... I fall prey to confusion.

Recognizing these and regaining balance takes a kind of patience diametrically opposed to the twenty-first-century's fierce tides, niggling distractions, or full-blown emergencies. The capacities required take us back to pausing, allowing this to flesh out and re-establish a connection with ground. Gotama, the renunciant monk we know as the Buddha, clearly saw the kind of mess we are in, visited by a deity who asked:

The inner tangle and the outer tangle –
This generation is entangled in a tangle.
And so I ask of Gotama this question:
Who succeeds in disentangling this tangle?[173]

With the foundation of non-harm and the development of clear understanding comes the reply: those who can know fear as fear, greed as greed, hatred as hatred, confusion as confusion, can disentangle the tangle. Seeing the fearful aspect, the greedy fabrication, the aversive self, the confused version, recognizing them as they come into being, stay awhile and fade, is the foundation for wiser responses.

Yanai reflects on times when a practice of turning towards difficulty was invaluable:

> There's an inner activism of sitting in the presence of what is hard to bear, and also to stand up in the face of external pressure, and yet to do so in a way of openness. A simple but quite direct example: 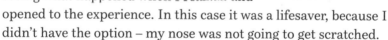 the first time I attached myself with a lock-on device to two other people (which meant I couldn't move), my nose started itching. I've spent time in meditation saying to myself, 'Look, you could scratch your nose, but right now why don't you see what happens when you don't?' and seeing what happened when I relaxed and opened to the experience. In this case it was a lifesaver, because I didn't have the option – my nose was not going to get scratched.
>
> Sometimes a situation of disruption will attract aggression, verbal or physical. Things might turn out to be really unpleasant; even when the risk is minimized there are always risks in a situation that involves multiple people and some degree of pressure. As much as possible my practice is to go there with an open heart. That openheartedness is part of equanimity, but it's also the fruit of equanimity.
>
> The first time I was arrested the officer came towards me, made eye contact, and said, 'My, you have a lovely smile!' (I acknowledge my high degree of privilege in this situation, as someone who passes as white, and is a middle-aged, middle-class, cisgender male.) That wasn't the first interaction I expected with the police when blocking a bridge in London. Being at peace with anticipating aggression allowed me to stay in my heart. That's one of the key elements of protection that equanimity offers.

Conflict

Sometimes our greatest challenges in the relational sphere lie in finding
steadiness with those who have different opinions, our nearest and
dearest, or those with whom we share a common cause. Yanai describes
the pain involved in this:

> One might assume the challenges might be in meeting the
> opposition. But there is a range of views and approaches in any
> community. I notice the tendency for people to get polarized and
> sometimes conflictual. It's one of the painful elements. To be able
> to say, 'There isn't going to be a way we all agree, and we will feel
> frustrated or reactive or judgemental towards others, despite
> sharing common cause.' That's a place that's tested my equanimity.
> Having reference to one's best intention, trusting that everyone is
> doing their best, is a great support.

Mulling over the theme of conflict I turn to Tchiyiwe to ask about her
experience. She acknowledges that conflict is inevitable, particularly in
the social-justice field, and, as we talk, she pauses for a beat or two, and
then her words return to a key foundation of compassion:

> I listen a lot. I try as much as possible to listen to what's being felt.
> I try to listen to what is being said, and what is not being said.
> There's always something other than what is being said and I want
> to respect that. I try to listen beyond the voice to what the deeper
> tension is. I may not be understanding you properly. I sit back, I
> try and listen so that I'm measured about how I respond. It doesn't

always work, but it has helped me go a long way.

It's not always that people play to their egos; they might be feeling insecure about things beyond the conversation you're having, or the issues you're dealing with. It helps to have that kind of awareness.[174]

CREATIVE EXPLORATION

Bring to mind a minor disagreement or conflict. How can the images you've gathered for steadiness and balance support you in finding a wider perspective?

Shoreline

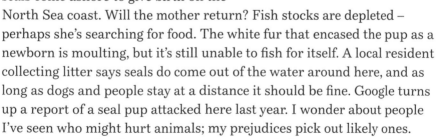

At low tide we find a seal pup lying on the rocks. A metre and a half long, it raises its head, yaps, and stares at us. Google says it's usual for pups to be left on their own. Don't get too close. It's almost two months before grey seals come ashore to give birth on the North Sea coast. Will the mother return? Fish stocks are depleted – perhaps she's searching for food. The white fur that encased the pup as a newborn is moulting, but it's still unable to fish for itself. A local resident collecting litter says seals do come out of the water around here, and as long as dogs and people stay at a distance it should be fine. Google turns up a report of a seal pup attacked here last year. I wonder about people I've seen who might hurt animals; my prejudices pick out likely ones.

It's easy to break one's heart over a stranded seal pup. Out of its natural element, unable to move. The compassion thought-police waver between 'You always want to ignore things when something must be done!' and 'You take too much responsibility for things beyond your control.'

Next day the worried one is still in the driving seat. More googling reveals there are two kinds of seal in this area: grey and common. Common seals are the least common: they have different-shaped heads, are smaller, their breeding season begins earlier, and pups can swim soon after birth. We've seen a common seal, probably an adolescent.

Anxiety settles; I've constructed a doom-laden picture. My mind bounces into a more hopeful relationship with experience. The optimistic version of myself takes shape; perhaps I can forget about seals for now.

Reading more widely I learn that common seals have declined by 50 per cent since 2000 due to unknown causes. Despair worms its way back in. The depressed self comes into being.

I also find researchers' blogs patiently documenting seal populations, and watch a video of a seal giving birth, her rolling contractions, the slippery, pulsating newborn as it emerges, mother and pup nuzzling each other, the tide coming in, mother encouraging pup to begin swimming.

There is a narrow viewpoint contracted around and co-arising with a fixed sense of self, always lacking the full information. And there is a bigger picture. It's true that something must and can be done, but the voices of denial and despair have contracted and diminished my ability to do it.

I resolve to walk the shoreline again and pay more attention. To look out for the fishing debris that can harm seals. To support charities that protect marine wildlife.

Yanai speaks to the theme of witnessing and vulnerability:

The ability to bear witness to something terrible and also preventable is really hard. One can bow more easily to those things – like mortality – that seem terrible but that we understand to be inevitable. Equanimity provides the capacity to see there is harm that is *not* inevitable, and yet understand one may not have the capacity, even with others, to address it. It provides the space to breathe with and grieve, to honour one's sorrow and not be completely subsumed by it. Equanimity arises from contemplating the fact that we can't determine the outcome. There's a vulnerability to really sit with that.

Making peace with the truth that not everyone gets to enjoy a full span of healthy life, not humans, not other living things. This has always been so, for reasons of accident, or illness, and

tragically also through injustice. To
contemplate this is to invite the
support of equanimity: 'There is no
certainty, but what's possible for me
to contribute in this circumstance?'
I can make a difference, even if
it's that I've aligned my heart and
done what I could. Even if the outer
circumstance doesn't change, in a way
at a spiritual level it does.

Zen master Yun-Men was asked, 'What is the highest, most profound teaching of this path?' He replied, 'An appropriate response.'

Death and loss are part of life, yet many – due to social, cultural, or geographic location – are shielded from it. Shielded too from the losses and devastation that this era brings. When we wake up to these, and when our personal sorrows come knocking, they shake us. Collective support for facing loss, such as the Death Café movement, helps to undo the taboos around mortality. Much creative climate action puts public rituals of mourning centre stage.

Grief is an appropriate and necessary response to our times. Unwinding from the fog of denial, we can learn to grieve in ways that sustain and support compassion rather than depleting it. Grief without the trappings of fear and shame can be like a birth: contractions of pain that spasm through the body, with their own timescale and pathways, that leave no room for anything else, and bring the release of sobbing and trembling.

When allowed to flow, grief can blossom into other forms – a sense of awe, an intimacy with life's rawness and beauty, a sharpening of intention. In the Buddha's final sickness, as he approached death, Ananda was desolate, leaning on a doorpost, weeping.

Enough, Ananda! Do not grieve, do not lament! For have I not taught from the very beginning that with all that is dear and beloved there must be change, separation, and severance? Of that which is born, come into being, compounded, and subject to decay, how can one say: 'May it not come to dissolution!'? There can be no such state of things.[175]

The Buddha did not console him, though perhaps there was tenderness in his voice, as he continued by praising Ananda for his devotion and kindness, and encouraging him to focus on his own practice.

In the process of giving up a view of all phenomena as fixed and permanent, much can happen between 'giving up' and 'no anxiety'. In this gap – that may feel more like a crevasse – live the skills of honouring and expressing grief, rather than bypassing it.

Grief Tending in Community is part of a movement to create ways in which grief is welcome and collectively held, in the knowledge that absence of spaces to grieve diminishes joy, love, and resilience. This movement honours the work of Sobunfu and Malidoma Somé, from the Dagara people of Burkina Faso, their generosity and legacy in sharing the wisdom of naming, tending, and giving collective space for grief.[176]

CREATIVE EXPLORATION

What forms do your despairing and hopeful selves take? How do you recognize them?

What images do you have for something you can lean into that is deeper than the winds of hope and despair?

How do you honour grief?

Illusion of self

In February 1950, Albert Einstein wrote a letter of consolation to a grieving father named Robert S. Marcus, political director of the World Jewish Congress, whose young son had died of polio. He reflected:

A human being is part of a whole, called by us the 'Universe', a part limited in time and space. They experience themself, their thoughts and feelings, as something separated from the rest – a kind of optical delusion of their consciousness. This delusion is a kind of prison for us, restricting us to our personal desires and to affection for a few persons nearest us. Our task must be to free ourselves from this

prison by widening our circles of compassion to embrace all living
creatures and the whole of nature in its beauty.[177]

The loss of a child is agonizing, yet what Einstein ventures to point to is
the way in which deepest sorrow can open us to what is universal.

It is said that in the mind of wisdom there is no separation
between the one who offers compassion and the one who receives it.
This aspiration sounds lovely, but it contradicts most of our sensory
experience. It runs counter to the felt sense that we are different
and separate from other beings, particularly other human beings.
Usually how we experience this difference is through conceiving of and
perceiving ourselves as either superior to, inferior to, or the same as
others. Each of these views rests on a delusion that we are intrinsically
a stable, unchanging entity. When we don't recognize ourselves, through
psychological distress, or because drugs, alcohol, or other substances
have distorted our perceptions, it can be profoundly disturbing. Even
on a mundane daily level, our self-views can be regularly shaken. I look
in the mirror and recognize myself at the same time as feeling surprised
that the person I see is dissimilar to the internalized sense of self.

Questioning and examining a fixed sense of 'I, me, and mine' is not
an end in itself. It is a means to freedom, to finding the heart's release
from conditioned reactivity, and habitual pushes and pulls – a freedom to
rest in a dynamic spaciousness that is fluid and flavoured with creativity
and possibility. In the closing lines of the *Metta Sutta*, freedom comes
in part from 'not holding to fixed views', and, with a pure heart and
clarity of vision, the 'self' is not born again. Aside from a metaphysical
interpretation, this points to freedom from coming into being for the
despairing one, the hopeful self, the 'better or worse than' construct, the
narrow identity that is tied to certain outcomes.

These lines also point to the ways in which the development of
upekkha and the other brahma-viharas leads to the peace and freedom
of *samadhi* or collectedness. Analayo writes that their 'boundless nature
offers an easy entry point into the boundless experiences of infinite space
and infinite consciousness',[178] and 'a temporary liberation of the mind
can be experienced already with lesser degrees of concentration.'[179]

How does a perspective of not-self protect us from the disconnect
that leads to pity, and from the severing of connection that fuels suffering
and overwhelm?

I ask Yanai to respond to this. He says:

No set of circumstances, conditions, or outcomes ultimately separates us from our deepest nature or removes us from our deeply connected and interwoven participation in life. We shut down or disconnect when we get caught in reactivity. Equanimity expresses an understanding of that deeper connection; there's a transparency that comes with it, allowing things to pass through, understanding that in the end conditions do not define or limit us in ultimate terms. And yet in the realm of our human lives they are what we engage with.

Joseph Goldstein describes how his meditation practice was transformed by a subtle grammatical shift from the active-voice construction to the passive voice. He started to reframe experience, instead of 'I'm hearing' or 'I'm thinking', shifting to 'Sounds being known', 'Thoughts being known'. This loosens the most subtle level of attachment, the identification with consciousness, with a fixed self who is the fount of knowing, the origin of awareness: The One Who Is Aware.[180] What happens when, instead of 'I'm breathing', there's a sense of breathing being known, or simply a body being breathed? Can this bring relief, lightness, liberation? Novelist Tom Robbins writes, 'human beings were invented by water as a device for transporting itself from one place to another.'[181] Life moves itself through us; a thought is thinking itself. Recall what happens when the carriage next to our train begins to move, giving the impression that we're moving. Perhaps we're under that kind of illusion all the time.

Sometimes illness shifts the perception of self:

Nausea and heat combine
to make the day come from left field
as if I woke not fitting the frame
a half-step to the side of my life.

I get out the sewing machine
and become a person
who pins fabric
and loads bobbins with thread.[182]

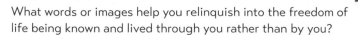

CREATIVE EXPLORATION

What words or images help you relinquish into the freedom of life being known and lived through you rather than by you?

Poetry on the street

Near the railway station I meet Andy.[183] From past conversations I've learned he used to be a chef, that he's fighting addiction, trying to stay away from bad influences, and waiting for help from the council. Sometimes he's selling the *Big Issue*, sometimes not. Today he brings out a folder and shows me his poems. A worker at the day centre has encouraged him to write. He lights up when he reads them to me. I light up too. The barriers get thinner: the giver–the receiver; the person with means–the person without. We talk about the writing process. Our shared interest dissolves my assumptions. It does not lessen the reality that the conditions of his life have left him vulnerable, and that the accident of birth has protected me from things that have harmed him.

A job lost, relationship breakup, bills unpaid, eviction, addiction, illness, and what we take for granted disintegrates. Tracking my responses in the city streets, I notice that when there's busyness in the mind the tendency to ignore people who are begging or homeless grows stronger. When anxiety is amplified, the separation between self and other strengthens. There is power in the simple intention to not hurry and to allow time to stop and talk. And I see how I'm encouraged to stop when I see others stopping, offering food, or buying a *Big Issue*. We give each other permission to break the spell.

Letting be

Dedication to the wellbeing of all life including ourselves need not be strained or arise from sacrificial or puritanical motivations. It can be supported by getting out of the way, recognizing the constructions that make compassion brittle. I run in the morning lanes, through rain, mist, and sunshine. Legs and lungs know how to do this. I point them in the right direction and let running do running. When conditioned, constricted selves are eased out of the way, compassion can enact itself, co-arising with our intentions, unfolding like day follows night. Fed by rest, metta, joy, and steadiness, it becomes part of a virtuous circle. In *The Merchant of Venice*, Shakespeare gives this speech to Portia disguised as the lawyer Balthazar, as she pleads with Shylock to save Antonio's life:

> The quality of mercy is not strained.
> It droppeth as the gentle rain
>   from heaven
> Upon the place beneath. It is twice
>   blest:
> It blesseth him that gives and him
>   that takes.[184]

Like this vision of mercy, in the right conditions compassion naturally unfolds in all directions. Whatever the external result might be, we ourselves are changed, are blessed.

Equanimity is sometimes defined as letting go of outcomes, an embodied realization that I may care deeply but each person is the owner and heir of their actions, and another's life is beyond my control. Letting another be as they are. Letting life be as it is, not from disconnection or fear of acting but with full-hearted engagement and the trembling that can respond to vulnerability. Compassion can be sustained only if it is allowed to ebb and flow as a natural opening of care and connection that emerges when the blocks of habit patterns and reactivity dissolve.

As our conversation draws to a close, Yanai and I speak about the relationship between equanimity and compassion.

> When encountering something painful, harmful, or unjust, the inner experience is deeply distressing and unwanted, and so the urge to

act can come from a wish to get rid of it. However, true compassion doesn't come out of an unwillingness to encounter suffering or injustice. Equanimity gives us the space and capacities to handle the suffering we might experience in the presence of another's suffering. It is the ground from which true compassion arises. There's a greater possibility that the action might be informed not by the wish to get rid of our own discomfort but out of finding the best possible way to respond.

CREATIVE EXPLORATION

 Guided Meditation – Letting be

Think of someone who is struggling or unwell right now, or a part of the world impacted by suffering. Finding some steadiness in yourself, take some slower breaths, experiment with offering both the wholeheartedness of compassion and the steadiness of equanimity, using this phrase or your own:

> I care for this deeply, and I let it be.

What arises?

Life's lineage

We know our lives will end; we don't know how or when. Everything we have and everyone we know will leave us or be left by us. The flowers will keep blooming, the rain will fall. The abandoned places of the world and of the human heart will endeavour to be reclaimed by boundless expressions of life. Forsake grand gestures, performative acts. Seek the quietude of offering what can be manifested in this moment, and the next. Touch into the extraordinary and improbable circumstance that any of us are here at all. What matters? What are you the conduit for? What is being brought forth? What will be forged in the crucible of grief, care, and joy?

In the storms and setbacks, as well as triumphs and delights, can there be, in Yanai's words:

> a certain dignified steadiness and peace that comes from having aligned one's life as best one can with what one believes to be true, skilful, and helpful.
>
> In the end it's not about the quantity, how long we live as a species or an individual, or even how long the living system of our planet is sustained, it's much more about the quality of what can be brought forth. That's something the heart can rest on, even in the most terrible of circumstances, that there is meaning and value in orienting towards what is wholesome and leaning one's actions towards what is possible.

In June 2016, the British MP Jo Cox was killed by a white supremacist. Jo was a principled, compassionate politician who had worked for Oxfam and Save the Children. Her maiden speech in Parliament included the words: 'We are far more united and have far more in common than that which divides us.' One year on from her murder, 'The Great Get Together' – a weekend of street parties, picnics, and concerts – marked the anniversary of Jo's death by celebrating her life and legacy. Invited to read poetry at one of these events, I wrote this sonnet, inspired by the scientific evidence that all known living organisms evolved from a common ancestor:

> In common – first breath, last, a pulse – put your fingers
> here on my throat where each beat's felt. Strangers
> or enemies we breathe each other's air and then
> the trees will keep on breathing when we've left.
> Four billion years since that first chemical reaction
> in the mud, and still we share some DNA
> with all that moves, is sensitive, takes in, gives out.
> So un-unique our flinch or flight from threat,
> the restless mix of wanting and not wanting to arrive,
> to sit in peace. In common – stomach's churn, the pull of dread,
> hate's easy reflex, the urge to say: *Them. Us.*
> And yet our fierce capacity to break at children's deaths,
> to fling ourselves at life, raise millions in an hour, to run,
> to run, to give up everything we have for what we love.

May the brahma-viharas become our anchors and dwelling places. May the inextinguishable love that befriends, enjoys, cares, and steadies – love that is almost always closer than we think – continue to open human hearts and minds, and bring us to freedom.

THE *METTA SUTTA*

From the *Sutta Nipata*, a group of discourses, many in verse, some
thought to be among the earliest Buddhist texts. This translation is by
the Amaravati Sangha, from *Chanting Book: Morning and Evening Puja
and Reflections* (Amaravati Publications, Hemel Hempstead 1994).
The Pali version and translations in many languages are available at
SuttaCentral.

> This is what should be done
> By one who is skilled in goodness,
> And who knows the path of peace:
> Let them be able and upright,
> Straightforward and gentle in speech.
>
> Humble and not conceited,
> Contented and easily satisfied,
> Unburdened with duties and frugal in their ways.
> Peaceful and calm, and wise and skilful,
> Not proud and demanding in nature.
>
> Let them not do the slightest thing
> That the wise would later reprove,
> Wishing: In gladness and in safety,
> May all beings be at ease.

Whatever living beings there may be,
Whether they are weak or strong, omitting none,
The great or the mighty, medium, short, or small,

The seen and the unseen,
Those living near and far away,
Those born and to-be-born,
May all beings be at ease.

Let none deceive another
Or despise any being in any state.
Let none through anger or ill-will
Wish harm upon another.

Even as a mother protects with her life
Her child, her only child,
So with a boundless heart
Should one cherish all living beings,
Radiating kindness over the entire world:

Spreading upwards to the skies,
And downwards to the depths,
Outwards and unbounded,
Freed from hatred and ill-will.

Whether standing or walking, seated,
Or lying down – free from drowsiness –
One should sustain this recollection.
This is said to be the sublime abiding.

By not holding to fixed views,
The pure-hearted one, having clarity of vision,
Being freed from all sense-desires,
Is not born again into this world.

Resource 2

REFLECTIONS FOR SUSTAINING COMPASSION IN DAILY LIFE

Five skilful guidelines for caring and non-harm

In the brahma-viharas of lovingkindness, compassion, sympathetic joy, and equanimity, we find nonharming conduct; in nonharming conduct, we find the brahma-viharas, the heavenly abodes, that are the revolutionary source of true happiness.

Sharon Salzberg[185]

Also known as the five ethical precepts or mindfulness trainings for lay practitioners, these are intended to be regularly spoken aloud, contemplated, and applied, not as commandments set in stone but as dynamic, responsive reflections on how to live compassionately and wisely, bringing a gift of fearlessness to ourselves and others.

Knowing how deeply our lives intertwine,
I undertake the training to refrain from harming living beings.
I aspire to respect and care for all life.

Knowing how deeply our lives intertwine,
I undertake the training to refrain from taking anything that is not
    freely offered to me.
I aspire to practise unconditional generosity.

Knowing how deeply our lives intertwine,
I undertake the training to refrain from misuse of sexual energy and
      the senses.
I aspire to relate to sexual energy and sensuality with respect and
      sensitivity.

Knowing how deeply our lives intertwine,
I undertake the training to refrain from untrue, harmful, or divisive
      speech.
I aspire to contribute to harmony through speaking and listening
      wisely.

Knowing how deeply our lives intertwine,
I undertake the training to refrain from intoxication that leads to
      carelessness.
I aspire to cultivate steadfastness and clarity.

These five trainings in non-harm and care are a foundation for
      wellbeing,
a vehicle for awakening,
and an offering to this world.

Five daily recollections

A contemporary version based on the practice (recommended by the
Buddha in AN 5.57) of reflecting frequently that I too am subject to
sickness, ageing, and death, that I will be parted from all things and
people I hold dear, and that I am the owner and heir of my actions.

Breathing gently, I lovingly remember
sickness, ageing, and death are part of life,
loss and separation are also unavoidable.
In the light of this, how may I live wisely, joyfully, and well?

Mealtime reflection

The need to eat and drink gives a regular chance to pause and reconnect with intentions. This is adapted from a Plum Village meal reflection.

> This food is a gift of the earth, the sky, numerous living beings, much hard work, much loving work.
>
> May I eat with mindfulness, with gratitude, with joy, with moderation.
>
> May I keep compassion alive by eating in such a way that reduces the suffering of living beings.
>
> May this food nourish me and my community, and my ideal of serving all beings.

Resource 3

SUSTAINING COMPASSION WITH OTHERS

A small sample of organizations mainly in the UK and Europe; many more are to be found in North America and internationally. Inclusion does not imply recommendation. With some exceptions these are groups that have contemplative, regenerative, creative, and/or social-justice approaches.

Awakening Joy. Online course led by Insight Meditation teacher James Baraz. https://www.awakeningjoy.info

Buddhists across Traditions. A UK-based Global Majority/BIPOC/ BPOC/BAME-centred collective uniting Buddhist and mindfulness groups in service of racial healing, social equity, and social justice. https://buddhistsacrosstraditions.org

ClimateCultures. Creative conversations for the Anthropocene. https://climatecultures.net

Climate.Emergence. Emotional & Ecological Wellbeing Strategies. Rest of Activism burnout prevention programme. https://www.climateemergence.co.uk

Colours of Compassion Sangha UK. For People of Colour / Black Asian Minority Ethnic / BPOC / Mixed Racial Heritages. Community with spiritual roots in tradition of Plum Village / Thich Nhat Hanh. https://plumvillage.uk/practice-groups/find-a-group/ colours-of-compassion/

DANCE: Dharma Action Network for Climate Engagement. https://www.facebook.com/groups/DharmaActionNetworkforClimateEngagement

The Dark Mountain Project. A cultural movement centred on creativity and the documenting of ecological, social, and cultural unravelling, through stories that can help us make sense of a time of disruption and uncertainty. https://dark-mountain.net

Death Café movement. https://deathcafe.com

Earth Vigil. http://www.earthvigil.co.uk

Eco Dharma Network UK. https://www.nbo.org.uk/eco-dharma-network/

Ekuthuleni. Meditation and eco retreats in southern France. https://ekuthuleni.wixsite.com/retreats

Extinction Rebellion (XR). Wellbeing and regenerative culture. https://extinctionrebellion.uk/act-now/resources/wellbeing/

XR community groups (including Afrikan heritage, BIPOC, religions and faiths, artists, writers). https://extinctionrebellion.uk/act-now/resources/communities/community-groups/

Grief Tending in Community. https://grieftending.org

Hope for the Future. Climate charity equipping communities, groups, and individuals across the UK to communicate the urgency of climate change with their local politicians. https://www.hftf.org.uk

iBme: Inward Bound Mindfulness Education. Groups and retreats for teens and young adults, including Communities of Colour, and Changemakers. https://ibme.org.uk (UK). https://ibme.com/about/ (US).

Julie's Bicycle. Creative climate action. https://juliesbicycle.com

KarunaNews. Amplifying the voices of collective compassion. https://www.karunanews.org

The Marginalian. Maria Popova's long-running site with mind-broadening and heart-lifting reflections spanning art, science, poetry, philosophy. https://www.themarginalian.org

Mindfulness and Social Change Network. https://mindfulnessandsocialchange.org

The Mindfulness Initiative. Bridging contemplative practice and public policy, championing the inner dimension of social change. https://www.themindfulnessinitiative.org

Movement for Change. Wellbeing and resilience support for charities and changemakers. https://www.movementforchange.co.uk

The Nap Ministry. https://thenapministry.com

The Natural Resilience Project. Celebrating the power, strength, and resilience of women living with irregular immigration status. Delivering nature-based workshops cultivating connections with ourselves and the natural world. https://www.naturalresilienceproject.com

NeuroSystemics. A Swiss-based global not-for-profit organization providing embodiment and relational trainings to enable a 'wiser, weller world'. https://neurosystemics.org

One Earth Sangha. A virtual EcoDharma centre. https://oneearthsangha.org

PAEAN: People's Alliance for Earth Action Now. https://sacredmountainsangha.org/paean-peoples-alliance-for-earth-action-now/

Positive News. https://www.positive.news

The Quadrangle. A not-for-profit organization and retreat centre promoting wellbeing and ecological regeneration. Currently offering retreats for NHS staff and other frontline workers. https://thequadrangle.co

Racial Justice Network – UK. https://racialjusticenetwork.co.uk

The Resilience Project UK. By youth, for youth. Empowering a generation of resilient changemakers. https://www.theresilienceproject.org.uk

SanghaSeva / Meditation in Action. Events that participate in humanitarian and ecological projects in ways that support deeper and more meaningful lives. https://www.sanghaseva.org

ServiceSpace (of which KarunaNews is one project). Volunteer-run organization, leveraging technology to encourage everyday people around the world to do small acts of service with the aim of fostering a culture of generosity. https://www.servicespace.org

Starter Culture. Collective Transformation from the Inside Out. https://starterculture.net

Triratna Earth Sangha. https://www.triratnaearthsangha.network

UBI Lab network. A worldwide network of citizens, researchers, and activists exploring the potential of universal basic income. https://www.ubilabnetwork.org

Ulex Project. A pan-European initiative to train changemakers in mindful awareness, resilience, and regenerative organizing. https://ulexproject.org

The Urban Mindfulness Foundation. Mindfulness trainings grounded in the alleviation of identity-based harm, and social and environmental injustice. https://www.urbanmindfulnessfoundation.co.uk

The Work That Reconnects Network. https://workthatreconnects.org

GLOSSARY

Ajahn (Thai): teacher, often used as the title of a senior monastic.

Ananda: the Buddha's cousin, and his attendant for the last twenty-five years of his life.

Anthropocene: the current geological age, in which humans have profoundly reshaped the planet and its biodiversity.

anukampa (Pali): compassion, literally 'trembling with'.

Avalokiteshvara: the bodhisattva who personifies compassion. Tibetans call him Chenrezig and believe he manifests as the Dalai Lama. In East Asia Avalokiteshvara becomes female and is known as Kwanyin in China and Kannon in Japan.

avijja (Pali): ignorance, confusion.

bhavana (Pali): cultivation, meditation, literally 'bringing into being'.

bhikkhu (Pali): 'alms mendicant', a fully ordained Buddhist monk.

bhikkuni (Pali): a fully ordained Buddhist nun.

BIPOC: black and brown people, indigenous people, and people of colour.

bodhisattva (Sanskrit): awakened being, one who aspires to become a Buddha for the purpose of helping others reach the same goal.

brahma-vihara (Pali): immeasurable, divine abode, boundless capacity.

Buddha (Pali/Sanskrit): one who has awakened.

Buddhaghosa: Indian-born scholar-monk who travelled to Sri Lanka in fifth-century CE, to translate into Pali the extensive Sinhalese commentaries preserved there.

citta (Pali, pronounced 'chitta'): the mind, particularly that aspect that is sensitive, is impacted, and responds.

Dhamma (Pali) / Dharma (Sanskrit): the teachings of the Buddhist tradition. With lower-case d can mean a belief system, a body of practices.

dukkha (Pali): painful or hard to bear, the spectrum of dis-ease, discontent, anguish, unsatisfactoriness.

Gotama: clan name for the historical Buddha.

***Jataka Tales*:** voluminous body of literature mainly concerning the previous births of Gotama Buddha in both human and animal form.

kalyana-mitta (Pali): wise, good friend.

kalyana-mittata (Pali): lovely, helpful friendship, often translated as spiritual friendship.

karuna (Pali/Sanskrit): compassion.

Mara: traditionally a demon, the personification of death, temptation, and evil.

metta (Pali): loving-kindness, goodwill, friendliness.

metta-bhavana (Pali): practice of developing loving-kindness.

***Metta Sutta*:** an early Buddhist text on loving-kindness.

mitta (Pali): friend.

mudita (Pali): joy, altruistic joy.

Nibbana (Pali) / Nirvana (Sanskrit): liberation, freedom from delusion and craving.

Nirodha (Pali): synonym for Nibbana.

Pali: literally 'text', the language in which early Buddhist teachings were written down. Does not have its own script, but can be written in, for example, Thai, Burmese, Sinhalese, roman script.

Pali canon: the standard collection of scriptures in the Theravada Buddhist tradition.

samadhi (Pali/Sanskrit): meditative absorption, collectedness.

sangha (Pali): community, originally those who commit themselves to monastic training.

Shantideva: Indian Buddhist monk, eighth century CE, who is said to have composed *A Guide to the Bodhisattva's Way of Life*.

sense organs: eye, ear, nose, tongue, skin, and (in the Buddhist framework) mind.

stupa (Sanskrit): hemispherical mound in which sacred relics of the Buddha or other revered person may be enshrined.

sukkha (Pali): wellbeing, ease, happiness.

sutta (Pali) / sutra (Sanskrit): a discourse attributed to the Buddha or one of his followers.

Thich Nhat Hanh (1926–2022): Vietnamese monk, teacher, social activist.

upekkha (Pali): equanimity, steadiness, balance.

vibhava tanha (Pali): the craving or thirst to not exist.

***Visudhimagga* (Pali)**: *The Path of Purification*, a systematic examination and condensation of Buddhist doctrine and meditation technique, written by Buddhaghosa in early fifth century CE.

ABBREVIATIONS

AN: *Anguttara Nikaya* (*Numerical Discourses*)
DN: *Digha Nikaya* (*Collection of Long Discourses*)
Ja: *Jataka Tales*
MN: *Majjhima Nikaya* (*Collection of Middle-Length Discourses*)
SN: *Samyutta Nikaya* (*Connected Discourses*)
Snp: *Sutta Nipata*, part of the *Khuddaka Nikaya* (*Minor Collection*)
Ud: *Udana* ('Inspired utterances'), part of the *Khuddaka Nikaya*
Vis: *Visuddhimagga*

Translations can be found at:
Access to Insight. Readings in Theravada Buddhism.
https://www.accesstoinsight.org
SuttaCentral. Early Buddhist texts, translations, and parallels.
https://suttacentral.net

SELECTED REFERENCES AND FURTHER READING

Not all the texts listed here are cited in these pages. Works that inspired or helped to shape the project are also included.

Tsultrim Allione, *Feeding Your Demons: Ancient Wisdom for Resolving Inner Conflict*, Little, Brown and Company, New York 2008.

Analayo, *Compassion and Emptiness in Early Buddhist Meditation*, Windhorse Publications, Cambridge 2015.

James Baraz and Shoshana Alexander, *Awakening Joy*, Parallax Press, Berkeley, CA, 2013.

Stephen Batchelor, *Living with the Devil: A Meditation on Good and Evil*, Penguin Books, London 2004.

Tara Brach, *Radical Acceptance: Embracing Your Life with the Heart of a Buddha*, Bantam Books, New York 2003.

Tara Brach, *Radical Compassion: Learning to Love Yourself and Your World with the Practice of RAIN*, Penguin Random House, New York 2020.

Jamie Bristow, Rosie Bell, and Christine Wamsler, 'Reconnection: meeting the climate crisis inside out. Research and policy report', The Mindfulness Initiative and LUCSUS, 2022.

adrienne maree brown, *Emergent Strategy: Shaping Change, Changing Worlds*, AK Books, Chico, CA, 2017.

Rob Burbea, *Seeing That Frees: Meditations on Emptiness and Dependent Arising*, Hermes Amara Publications, West Ogwell 2014.

Dalai Lama, Desmond Tutu, and Douglas Abrams, *The Book of Joy*, Hutchinson, London 2016.

The Dhammapada, trans. Gil Fronsdal, Shambhala, Boston, MA, 2005.

Eugene Ellis, *The Race Conversation: An Essential Guide to Creating Life-Changing Dialogue*, Confer Books, London 2021.

Malena Ernman, Greta Thunberg, Beata Ernman, and Svante Thunberg, *Our House Is on Fire: Scenes of a Planet and a Family in Crisis*, Penguin, London 2021.

Christina Feldman, *Boundless Heart: The Buddhist Path of Kindness, Compassion, Joy, and Equanimity*, Shambhala, Boulder, CO, 2018.

Christina Feldman, *Compassion: Listening to the Cries of the World*, Rodmell Press, Berkeley, CA, 2005.

Cal Flyn, *Islands of Abandonment: Life in the Post-Human Landscape*, HarperCollins, London 2021.

Gil Fronsdal, *The Buddha before Buddhism: Wisdom from the Early Teachings*, Shambhala, Boulder, CO, 2016.

Natalie Goldberg, *Writing Down the Bones: Freeing the Writer Within*, Shambhala, Boston, MA, 1986.

Staci Haines, *The Politics of Trauma*, North Atlantic Books, Berkeley, CA, 2019.

Joan Halifax, *Standing at the Edge: Finding Freedom Where Fear and Courage Meet*, Flatiron Books, New York 2019.

Claudia Hammond, *The Art of Rest: How to Find Respite in the Modern Age*, Canongate, Edinburgh 2019.

Byung-Chul Han, *The Disappearance of Rituals: A Topology of the Present*, Polity Press, Cambridge 2020.

Tricia Hersey, *Rest Is Resistance: A Manifesto*, Little, Brown Spark, Boston, MA, 2022.

Ruth King, *Mindful of Race: Transforming Racism from the Inside Out*, Sounds True, Boulder, CO, 2018.

Bessel van der Kolk, *The Body Keeps the Score: Mind, Brain and Body in the Transformation of Trauma*, Penguin, London 2015.

Jack Kornfield, *A Path With Heart: A Guide Through the Perils and Promises of Spiritual Life*, Rider, London 1994.

Olivia Laing, *Funny Weather: Art in an Emergency*, Picador, London 2021.

Anthea Lawson, *The Entangled Activist: Learning to Recognise the Master's Tools*, Perspectiva Press, London 2021.

Kaira Jewel Lingo, *We Were Made for These Times: Ten Lessons for Moving Through Change, Loss and Disruption*, Parallax Press, Berkeley, CA, 2021.

Audre Lorde, 'Eye to eye: Black women, hatred, and anger', in *Sister Outsider: Essays and Speeches*, Ten Speed Press, New York 2007, pp.154–63.

Joanna Macy and Chris Johnstone, *Active Hope: How to Face the Mess We're in Without Going Crazy*, New World Library, Novato, CA, 2012.

Rhonda Magee, *The Inner Work of Racial Justice: Healing Ourselves and Transforming Our Communities Through Mindfulness*, TarcherPerigee, New York 2019.

Zenju Earthlyn Manuel, *The Deepest Peace: Contemplations from a Season of Stillness*, Parallax Press, Berkeley, CA, 2020.

Zenju Earthlyn Manuel, *The Way of Tenderness: Awakening through Race, Sexuality, and Gender*, Wisdom Publications, Somerville, MA, 2015.

Alastair McIntosh, *Riders on the Storm: The Climate Crisis and the Survival of Being*, Birlinn, Edinburgh 2020.

Resmaa Menakem, *My Grandmother's Hands: Racialized Trauma and the Pathway to Mending Our Hearts and Bodies*, Penguin, London 2021.

Lama Rod Owens, *Love and Rage: The Path of Liberation Through Anger*, North Atlantic Books, Berkeley, CA, 2020.

Maria Popova, *The Marginalian*, https://www.themarginalian.org/about/.

Loretta Pyles, *Healing Justice: Holistic Self-Care for Change Makers*, Oxford University Press, Oxford 2018.

Sarah Jaquette Ray, *A Field Guide to Climate Anxiety: How to Keep Your Cool on a Warming Planet*, University of California Press, Oakland, CA, 2020.

Ryokan, *Between the Floating Mist: Poetry of Ryokan*, trans. Dennis Maloney, White Pine Press, Buffalo, NY, 2009.

Ryokan, *One Robe One Bowl: The Zen Poetry of Ryokan*, trans. John Stevens, Weatherhill, Boston, MA, 2006.

Sharon Salzberg, *Lovingkindness: The Revolutionary Art of Happiness*, Shambhala, Boston, MA, 1995.

Shantideva, *A Guide to the Bodhisattva's Way of Life*, trans. Stephen Batchelor, Library of Tibetan Works and Archives, Dharamsala 1979.

Ajahn Sucitto and Nick Scott, *Where Are You Going? A Pilgrimage on Foot to the Buddhist Holy Places, Part 1: Rude Awakenings*, Cittaviveka Monastery free edition, 2010.

Thanissara, *Time to Stand Up: The Buddha's Life and Message through Feminine Eyes*, North Atlantic Books, Berkeley, CA, 2015.

Thich Nhat Hanh, *Being Peace*, Rider, London 1992.

David Treleaven, *Trauma-Sensitive Mindfulness: Practices for Safe and Transformative Healing*, Norton, New York 2018.

Robin Wall Kimmerer, *Braiding Sweetgrass: Indigenous Wisdom, Scientific Knowledge, and the Teachings of Plants*, Penguin, London 2020.

Matty Weingast and Bhikkhuni Anandabodhi, *The First Free Women: Original Poems Inspired by the Early Buddhist Nuns*, Shambhala, Boulder, CO, 2021.

Rev. angel Kyodo williams and Lama Rod Owens, with Jasmine Syedullah, *Radical Dharma: Talking Race, Love, and Liberation*, North Atlantic Books, Berkeley, CA, 2016.

Larry Yang, *Awakening Together: The Spiritual Practice of Inclusivity and Community*, Wisdom Publications, Somerville, MA, 2017.

ACKNOWLEDGEMENTS

I recognize that my perspectives reflect the limitations and unconscious biases of a white, cisgender, middle-aged, able-bodied woman from a materially and educationally privileged background. Untangling from these biases is crucial to a path of wisdom and compassion, and I welcome feedback. This book was written on the soil of England, a country rooted in and formed from the toil and stewardship of many peoples and many layers of migration, part of a nation whose relative prosperity is the result of stealing, appropriating, colonizing, and exploiting the people and resources of other lands.

As a Western practitioner of the Dharma, I honour the preservation of Buddhist teachings and practice by monastic and lay practitioners in global-majority countries. Countless people in Asian countries have kept the wheel turning through their practice and generosity, and have made it possible for others to tread this path.

No creative work has just one progenitor; this book is the fruit of countless sources of generosity. My teachers, particularly at Bodhi College, Gaia House, and other Insight Meditation centres, have given invaluable guidance over many years. Many of their insights planted seeds for this project, but all errors and misinterpretations are mine alone.

A grant from Hemera Foundation's Tara Project for women teachers provided space and time to write the first drafts. Thank you to Lizzie Fuller, Sean Kloppenburg, and the Hemera trustees for their encouragement. Enthusiasm, dedication, and support from Dhammamegha Leatt, Michelle Bernard, Dhatvisvari, Tarajyoti, the readers, and the editorial board at Windhorse have carried the book to completion. Working with artist Emma Burleigh and designer Francesca Romano has brought the joys of creative collaboration right into the heart of the project.

Jo Burn helped set the wheel in motion before the first words were even written. Val Regan, Catherine McGee, and Jassy Denison read early drafts of some sections and gave invaluable feedback; Mary Ann Orme read both early and final drafts, and I'm grateful for her detailed and insightful comments.

I am blessed with good friends and companions on the path; heartfelt thanks to Zohar, Nathan, Jaya, Kareem, Esther, and Yanai, whose reflections gave the book its lifeblood. I'm grateful to Tchiyiwe Chihana, Milla Gregor, and 'Bow' for their essential contributions.

Thank you to the dharma siblings with whom I've discussed many angles of the brahma-viharas: Sophie Boyer, Becca Crane, Juliet Denham, Alison Evans, Bernat Font Clos, Katrin Auf der Heyde, Isabel Palma Hohmann, Gerit Stöcklmair, Julia Wallond, and everyone on the Bodhi College Teacher Training Programme.

Longtime friends are a continual source of joy. Shout out to the Old Pals, the Beautiful Beasties, the LASSes, the iBme crew, and neighbours and community in the Hope Valley. A deep bow to the meditation communities I'm privileged to know and serve, and all the retreatants and meditators whose questions and practice inspire and sustain me.

I'm immensely grateful for libraries, the few remaining, often endangered, non-commercial public spaces on the high street where free resources are available to all. As I wrote the final drafts in Torbay's libraries, librarians patiently tracked down books and references for me. In midwinter times of economic hardship, they were also offering hot drinks, warm clothing, and a warm welcome to anyone in need. Compassion in action.

My younger brother Adam died when I was partway through the project. Though he shared with me an engrained scepticism towards religion and dogma, the Dharma touched his life in his last months. The book is also dedicated to his tender heart, his love of nature, and his passion for Palestinian freedom and justice.

The support and encouragement of my partner Fiona Outram make everything possible. Her kind heart, bright mind, and quick wit sustain me, and remind me, time and again, that there is no way to love – love is the way.

River Wolton
Hope Valley, March 2023

NOTES

INTRODUCTION

1 Alastair McIntosh, *Riders on the Storm: The Climate Crisis and the Survival of Being*, Birlinn, Edinburgh 2020, p.xi.

2 Sinéad O'Connor, 'Black boys on mopeds', from *I Do Not Want What I Haven't Got* (1990).

3 Interview with Mónica Gomery, *Palette Poetry* (October 2022), available at https://www.palettepoetry.com/2022/09/27/occupational-hazards/, accessed on 27 March 2023.

4 *The Guardian* email appeal to supporters, September 2022.

5 Reports from the Intergovernmental Panel on Climate Change (IPCC) give degrees of confidence (low, medium, high) for whether different scenarios are likely or unlikely. Predictions of temperature rise vary widely. The full spectrum can be found in *IPCC Special Report on Climate Change: The Ocean and the Cryosphere*; the four emissions scenarios discussed in this report are usefully summarized in McIntosh, *Riders on the Storm*, pp.23–6.

6 See https://spacenews.com/space-junk-in-orbit-is-bad-enough-but-on-mars/, accessed on 27 March 2023.

7 E. Alison Holman, Dana Rose Garfin, and Roxane Cohen Silver, 'Media's role in broadcasting acute stress following the Boston Marathon bombings', *PNAS* 111:1 (9 December 2013), pp.93–8. I'm grateful to Oliver Burkeman, and his podcast 'Living with the news', for pointing me to this research.

8 Roshi Joan Halifax, 'Finding buoyancy amidst despair', 'On being' podcast with Krista Tippett (12 October 2017), available at https://onbeing.org/programs/joan-halifax-finding-buoyancy-amidst-despair/, accessed on 27 March 2023.

9 Roshi Joan Halifax, *Standing at the Edge: Finding Freedom Where Fear and Courage Meet*, Flatiron Books, New York 2019, p.2.

10 Jason Hickel, 'Quantifying national responsibility for climate breakdown: an equality-based attribution approach for carbon dioxide emissions in excess of the planetary boundary', *Lancet Planetary Health* 4:9 (September 2020), pp.e399–404, available at https://doi.org/10.1016/S2542-5196(20)30196-0, accessed on 27 March 2023.

11 M. Ballew et al., 'Which racial/ethnic groups care most about climate change?', available at https://climatecommunication.yale.edu/publications/race-and-climate-change/, accessed on 27 March 2023.

12 C. Hickman et al., 'Climate anxiety in children and young people and their beliefs about government responses to climate change: a global survey', *Lancet Planetary Health* 5:12 (December 2021), pp.e863–73, available at https://doi.org/10.1016/S2542-5196(21)00278-3, accessed on 27 March 2023.

13 '[In 2021–2] [t]he adult social care workforce continued to be made up of around 82% female workers, the average age was 45 (with 28% aged 55 and over), 23% of the workforce had black, Asian and minority ethnicity and 16% had a non-British nationality'. See https://www.skillsforcare.org.uk/adult-social-care-workforce-data/Workforce-intelligence/publications/national-information/The-state-of-the-adult-social-care-sector-and-workforce-in-England.aspx, accessed on 27 March 2023.

14 Christine Brown Wilson *et al.*, 'The best care is like sunshine: accessing older people's experiences of living in care homes through creative writing', *Activities, Adaptation & Aging* 31:1 (2011), pp.1–20.

15 See https://www.carersuk.org/policy-and-research/key-facts-and-figures/, accessed on 27 March 2023.

16 Sophie Hardach, 'The German clinics for burnt-out parents' (8 March 2023), https://www.bbc.com/future/article/20230228-the-german-clinics-for-burnt-out-parents, accessed on 27 March 2023.

17 From *A Gallon of Love: Creative Writing by Carers*, ed. River Wolton, unpublished pamphlet, written at Buxton Library, Derbyshire County Council (2009).

18 Joanna Macy and Chris Johnstone, *Active Hope: How to Face the Mess We're in Without Going Crazy*, New World Library, Novato, CA, 2012, pp.26–33.

19 Conversation with Tchiyiwe Chihana (22 February 2023).

20 See https://climatecultures.net, accessed on 27 March 2023.

21 Olivia Laing, *Funny Weather: Art in an Emergency*, Picador, London 2021, p.8.

22 Emma L. Lawrance *et al.*, 'The impact of climate change on mental health and emotional wellbeing', *International Review of Psychiatry* 34:5 (2022), pp.443–98.

23 Ashlee Cunsolo *et al.*, 'Ecological grief and anxiety: the start of a healthy response to climate change?', *The Lancet Planetary Health* 4:7 (2020), pp.E261–3.

24 See https://www.alrowwad.org/en/, accessed on 27 March 2023.

25 Jamie Bristow *et al.*, 'Reconnection: meeting the climate crisis inside out – research and policy report', www.themindfulnessinitiative.org/reconnection, accessed on 27 March 2023.

26 See http://www.earthvigil.co.uk, accessed on 27 March 2023.

27 See https://www.theresilienceproject.org.uk, accessed on 27 March 2023.

28 Alaa' Al-Samarrai, 'Tackling climate change as stewards of our green earth', 'Hope for the Future' blog (October 2022), https://www.hftf.org.uk/blog/2022/10/21/tackling-climate-change-as-stewards-of-our-green-earth, accessed on 27 March 2023.

29 *The Dhammapada*, trans. Gil Fronsdal, Shambhala, Boston, MA, 2005, verses 33–5, p.9.

30 Joseph Goldstein recalling an observation made by his teacher Anagarika Munindra, in Joseph Goldstein, *Mindfulness: A Practical Guide to Awakening*, Sounds True, Boulder, CO, 2013, p.22.

31 Caroline Labow, 'How does language shape our climate restoration mission?' (1 October 2022), https://www.humansforabundance.com/post/how-does-language-shape-our-climate-restoration-mission, accessed on 27 March 2023.

32 Susie Dent, 'From respair to cacklefart: the joy of reclaiming long-lost positive words', *The Guardian* (26 December 2021), https://www.theguardian.com/commentisfree/2021/dec/26/respair-cacklefart-positive-words-english-language, accessed on 27 March 2023.

33 Robin Wall Kimmerer, *Braiding Sweetgrass: Indigenous Wisdom, Scientific Knowledge, and the Teachings of Plants*, Penguin, London 2020, p.x.

34 Longchenpa, from the *Trilogy of Finding Comfort and Ease*. I am grateful to John Peacock for his kind permission to use this translation, and for his teaching and reflections on it.

35 A translation of the *Metta Sutta* can be found on p.173.

36 *The Suttanipata and Commentaries*, trans. Bhikkhu Bodhi, Wisdom Publications, Somerville, MA, 2017, Pj II verses 251–2, p.583.

37 DN 13, *Tevijja (Three Knowledges) Sutta*.

38 MN 22, *Simile of the Snake*, trans. Bhikkhu Sujato. Licensed under Creative Commons Zero (CC0), available at https://suttacentral.net/mn22/en/sujato, accessed on 27 March 2023.

39 See below, p.170.

40 See below, p.103.

41 SN 45.2, *Upaddha Sutta*.

42 From 'The breeze at dawn', in *The Essential Rumi*, trans. Coleman Barks, Castle Books, Edison, NJ, 1997, p.36.

CHAPTER 1

43 Byung-Chul Han, *The Disappearance of Rituals: A Topology of the Present*, Polity Press, Cambridge 2020, pp.45–6.

44 Sangha: community of spiritual friends or like-minded people. Seva: selfless service, offering the best we have to give. See https://www.sanghaseva.org/infosanghaseva.html, accessed on 28 March 2023.

45 See http://anandwan.in, accessed on 28 March 2023.

46 A fragment from Plautus preserved by Aulus Gellius. Adapted from a quote available at https://www.laphamsquarterly.org/roundtable/monumental-timekeepers, accessed on 5 April 2023.

47 See https://thenapministry.com, accessed on 28 March 2023.

48 Tricia Hersey, *Rest Is Resistance: A Manifesto*, Little, Brown Spark, Boston, MA, 2022.

49 Quoted with the permission of Rahima Gambo.

50 See https://www.arestguide.com/volume/amanda-iheme, accessed on 28 March 2023.

51 Shantideva, *A Guide to the Bodhisattva's Way of Life*, trans. Stephen Batchelor, Library of Tibetan Works and Archives, Dharamsala 1979, ch.3, stanzas 18–22, p.22.

52 Ibid., ch.7, stanzas 31 and 67, pp.81 and 87.

53 Bessel van der Kolk, *The Body Keeps the Score: Mind, Brain and Body in the Transformation of Trauma*, Penguin, London 2015.

54 David Treleaven, *Trauma-Sensitive Mindfulness: Practices for Safe and Transformative Healing*, Norton, New York 2018.

55 For example: Staci Haines, *The Politics of Trauma*, North Atlantic Books, Berkeley, CA, 2019.

56 William Shakespeare, *Hamlet*, act 3, scene 1.

57 Quote adapted from Dogen's *Genjokoan*.

58 James Joyce, 'A painful case', in *Dubliners*, Grant Richards, London 1914, p.131.

59 From a Dharma talk given at Gaia House, October 2016. Quoted with Leela Sarti's permission.

60 River Wolton, '23 February', in *Year*, Smith/Doorstop, Sheffield 2022, p.25.

61 See https://www.movementforchange.co.uk, accessed on 28 March 2023.

62 Conversation with Milla Gregor (30 November 2022).

63 Zenju Earthlyn Manuel, *The Deepest Peace: Contemplations from a Season of Stillness*, Parallax Press, Berkeley, CA, 2020, pp.105–6.

64 'Inner deep listening and quiet still awareness', a reflection by Miriam Rose Ungunmerr available at https://www.miriamrosefoundation.org.au/dadirri/, accessed on 28 March 2023.

65 See https://www.commondreams.org/news/2020/09/15/groundbreaking-study-shows-deep-listening-over-100-times-more-effective-winning, accessed on 28 March 2023.

66 George Goehl podcast, 'To see each other', episode 2, available at https://peoplesaction.org/tseo-ep2/, accessed on 28 March 2023.

67 River Wolton, 'Statistics', in *The Purpose of Your Visit*, Smith/Doorstop, Sheffield 2009, p.24.

68 See https://www.gofundme.com/f/help-build-the-garden-of-hope-mindfulness-centre, accessed on 28 March 2023.

CHAPTER 2

69 Ja.vi.526 quoted at http://sdhammika.blogspot.com/2010/08/buddha-and-trees-ii.html, accessed on 28 March 2023.

70 Snp 1.8, *Metta Sutta*. The Pali text for this sutta, also known as the *Karaniya Metta Sutta*, together with many translations, is available at https://suttacentral.net/snp1.8, accessed on 28 March 2023.

71 In his translation of the commentary on the *Metta Sutta*, Bhikkhu Bodhi notes that although 'metta is derived from mitta ... "friendliness" conveys too casual a meaning and "good will" or "benevolence" may miss the emotional resonances of metta.' See *The Suttanipata and Commentaries*, p.1408.

72 River Wolton, '2 January', in *Year*, p.8.

73 MN 10, *Satipatthana Sutta*, trans. Bhikkhu Sujato. Licensed under Creative Commons Zero (CC0), available at https://suttacentral.net/mn10/en/sujato, accessed on 28 March 2023.

74 Wilfred Owen, 'Futility', written in May 1918, available at https://www.poetryfoundation.org/poems/57283/futility-56d23aa2d4b57, accessed on 28 March 2023.

75 Interview with Julia Butterfly Hill, 'Living on Earth', available at https://www.loe.org/shows/segments.html?programID=00-P13-00016&segmentID=1, accessed on 28 February 2023.

76 Lama Rod Owens, *Love and Rage: The Path of Liberation Through Anger*, North Atlantic Books, Berkeley, CA, 2020, pp.178–9.

77 Buddhaghosa, *The Path of Purification (Visuddhimagga)*, trans. Bhikkhu Nanamoli, Buddhist Publication Society Pariyatti Edition, Kandy 1999, p.289.

78 Ibid. (quoting SN 3.8 / Ud 5.1), p.290.

79 River Wolton, '16 January', in *Year*, p.12.

80 River Wolton, '31 January', in *Year*, p.17.

81 Larry Yang, *Awakening Together: The Spiritual Practice of Inclusivity and Community*, Wisdom Publications, Somerville, MA, 2017, p.167.

82 Ibid., pp.235–6.

83 Quote attributed to A.J. Muste.

84 Ryokan, *One Robe One Bowl: The Zen Poetry of Ryokan*, trans. John Stevens, Weatherhill, Boston, MA, 2006, p.56.

85 River Wolton, '15 December', in *Betweenity: Poems from a Three-Month Retreat* (self-published, 2019, no page numbers).

86 Audre Lorde, 'Eye to eye: Black women, hatred, and anger', in *Sister Outsider: Essays and Speeches*, Ten Speed Press, New York 2007, pp.154–63 (p.156).

87 SN 5.2, *With Soma*. Author's translation.

88 MN 119, *Kayagatasati Sutta*.

89 Snp 3.2, *Padhana Sutta*.

90 SN 36.6, *Sala Sutta*.

91 For detailed practices, including working with art, see Tsultrim Allione, *Feeding Your Demons: Ancient Wisdom for Resolving Inner Conflict*, Little, Brown and Company, New York 2008, pp.51–104.

92 For examples of working with the inner critic through writing, see River Wolton, 'Critic tango', in *Writing Works: A Resource Handbook for Therapeutic Writing Workshops and Activities*, ed. Gillie Bolton, Jessica Kingsley Publishers, London 2006, pp.176–80.

93 River Wolton, '15 September', in *Year*, p.98.

94 Thanissaro Bhikkhu, 'Reconciliation, right and wrong', available at https://www.dhammatalks.org/books/PurityOfHeart/Section0010.html, accessed on 28 March 2023.

95 Desmond and Mpho Tutu, 'On truth and reconciliation in the United States', audio recording in *Yes! Magazine* (31 May 2015).

96 MN 21, *The Simile of the Saw*, trans. Bhikkhu Nanamoli, in *The Middle Length Discourses of the Buddha: A Translation of the Majjhima Nikaya*, ed. Bhikkhu Bodhi, Wisdom Publications, Boston, MA, 1995, p.223.

97 Ruth King, *Mindful of Race: Transforming Racism from the Inside Out*, Sounds True, Boulder, CO, 2018, p.101.

98 Sharon Salzberg, *Lovingkindness: The Revolutionary Art of Happiness*, Shambhala, Boston, MA, 1995, p.30.

99 Christina Feldman, *Boundless Heart: The Buddhist Path of Kindness, Compassion, Joy, and Equanimity*, Shambhala, Boulder, CO, 2018, p.32.

CHAPTER 3

100 MN 19, *Dvedhavitakka Sutta*, trans. Bhikkhu Sujato. Licensed under Creative Commons Zero (CC0), available at https://suttacentral.net/mn19/en/sujato, accessed on 29 March 2023.

101 River Wolton, '17 November', in *Betweenity*.

102 Inward Bound Mindfulness Education UK, providing retreats and courses for teens and young adults. See https://ibme.org.uk, accessed on 29 March 2023.

103 Tara Brach, *Radical Acceptance: Embracing Your Life with the Heart of a Buddha*, Bantam Books, New York 2003, pp.5–23.

104 Mary Oliver, 'Wild geese', in *Wild Geese: Selected Poems*, Bloodaxe, Hexham 2004, p.21.

105 River Wolton, '5 May', in *Year*, p.53.

106 Jack Kornfield, 'Gratitude and wonder', available at https://jackkornfield.com/gratitude/, accessed on 29 March 2023.

107 'Take in the good', available at https://www.rickhanson.net/take-in-the-good/, accessed on 29 March 2023.

108 River Wolton, '2 November', in *Year*, p.116.

109 Conversation with 'Bow' (19 February 2023).

110 Summer Allen, 'The science of gratitude', available at https://ggsc.berkeley.edu/images/uploads/GGSC-JTF_White_Paper-Gratitude-FINAL.pdf, accessed on 29 March 2023, pp.4–5.

111 Ibid., p.25.

112 Ibid., p.56.

113 Ibid., p.56.

114 Caroline Criado Perez, *Invisible Women: Exposing Data Bias in a World Designed by Men*, Vintage Publishing, London 2020.

115 Ibid., p.49.

116 Dalai Lama, Desmond Tutu, and Douglas Abrams, *The Book of Joy*, Hutchinson, London 2016, pp.273–4.

117 A version of 'Eternity' by William Blake. Pronouns in the original poem are 'he/himself'.

118 These joy phrases, adapted from ones offered by Chris Cullen, are used with his permission.

CHAPTER 4

119 Manuel, *The Deepest Peace*, p.148.

120 Campaign to End Loneliness: see https://www.campaigntoendloneliness.org/the-facts-on-loneliness/, accessed on 29 March 2023.

121 River Wolton, '20 April' in *Year*, p.45.

122 Quoted with the permission of Melany Zarate from her presentation at 'Can Buddhism grow inclusive communities? Intersectionality of race, gender and sexuality', February 2022, organized by Buddhists across Traditions, available at https://youtu.be/xMMacaqzB98, accessed on 29 March 2023.

123 Dr Martin Luther King Jr, 'Massey Lecture 5', available at https://speakola.com/ideas/martin-luther-king-jr-interconnected-world-massey-5-1967, accessed on 29 March 2023.

124 Snp 1.8, *Metta Sutta*, translated from the Pali by the Amaravati Sangha, available at http://www.accesstoinsight.org/tipitaka/kn/snp/snp.1.08.amar.html, accessed on 28 February 29 March 2023. The Pali text of the *Metta Sutta* has gendered pronouns and nouns, for example, 'he/him', 'mother', and 'son', reflecting its historical and cultural context. In the Amaravati Sangha translation, *putta* (son) has been rendered as 'child', and instead of 'he/him' the pronouns 'one' and 'they' have been used throughout. Amaravati Publications request there to be no modifications of their translation, so the translation of *mata* as 'mother' rather than 'parent' has been reproduced in this extract, and in Resource 1 where the whole sutta is quoted. I have not found, or had the skill to make, a translation of the sutta that uses gender-neutral terms throughout, and, in the process, both questions the myth of innate motherly love, and reflects the

powerful, protective love that fathers and non-binary parents can feel towards their children. There is debate on how and when to adapt traditional texts; however I would argue that gender-neutral terms enable Dharma teachings to become accessible, embodied, and relevant in a contemporary context.

125 Thanissaro Bhikkhu interprets the meaning of this passage as protecting one's *friendliness* as a parent protects their child, rather than cultivating friendliness towards all beings. See https://www.accesstoinsight.org/lib/authors/thanissaro/metta_means_goodwill.html, accessed on 29 March 2023.

126 Moscone Milk Memorial 2008, available at https://youtu.be/LbXq0oU5osg, accessed on 29 March 2023.

127 Harry later lived in Manchester and a play about their life, *Mister Stokes: The Man-Woman of Manchester*, was performed there in 2016. I'm grateful to Sheffield City Council, Libraries, Archives and Information. See 'Sources for the study of the history of LGBT communities', available at https://www.sheffield.gov.uk/sites/default/files/docs/libraries-and-archives/archives-and-local-studies/research/LGBT%20Study%20Guide%20v2-9.pdf, accessed on 29 March 2023.

128 See https://www.outofthearchive.co.uk/resisters, accessed on 29 March 2023.

129 'Allies' and 'allyship' can be problematic terms. For some they signify separation rather than support. Konda Mason (speaking on the interrelated crises of climate, ecology, racial and social injustice): 'I want to dismiss the word "ally", it immediately creates separation. Injustice is everyone's issue.' Panel discussion at 'Buddhism and ecology summit', April 2022.

130 See https://workthatreconnects.org, accessed on 29 March 2023.

131 Alastair McIntosh, *Riders on the Storm: The Climate Crisis and the Survival of Being*, Birlinn, Edinburgh 2020, p.191.

132 River Wolton, '7 August', in *Year*, p.84.

133 'Karuna' is a Sanskrit and Pali word for 'compassion'. See https://www.karunavirus.org/en/about, accessed on 29 March 2023.

134 See https://www.standard.co.uk/news/politics/boris-johnson-queens-speech-cost-of-living-government-keir-starmer-b999205.html, accessed on 29 March 2023.

135 Life After Hate: see https://www.lifeafterhate.org, accessed on 29 March 2023.

136 'How to get through to white supremacists', available at https://youtu.be/-_BhX8bl9cY, accessed on 29 March 2023.

137 The Karpman Drama Triangle, one map of a type of destructive interaction that can occur among people in conflict.

138 I'm grateful for this insight to Gil Fronsdal and his Dharma talks on audiodharma.org, particularly the series on 'Care'.

139 Analayo, *Compassion and Emptiness in Early Buddhist Meditation*, Windhorse Publications, Cambridge 2015, p.13.

140 Adrienne Rich, from 'Integrity', in *A Wild Patience Has Taken Me This Far: Poems 1978–1981*, Norton, New York 1993, p.11.

141 River Wolton, '7 March', in *Year*, p.31.

142 I'm grateful to Dharma teachers Anushka Fernandopulle and Bonnie Duran, whose Gaia House online retreat 'Decolonising the mind and cultivating the causes of happiness' in June 2020 inspired much of this section.

143 'Global cotton connections', available at https://www.derwentvalleymills.org/discover/derwent-valley-mills-research/recent-research/global-cotton-connections/, accessed on 29 March 2023.

144 See the work of Catherine Hall, Emerita Professor of History and Chair of the Centre for the Study of the Legacies of British Slavery, University College London. See https://www.ucl.ac.uk/lbs/project/staff/, accessed on 29 March 2023.

145 Kris Manjapra, 'When will Britain face up to its crimes against humanity?', *The Guardian* (29 March 2018), available at https://www.theguardian.com/news/2018/mar/29/slavery-abolition-compensation-when-will-britain-face-up-to-its-crimes-against-humanity, accessed on 29 March 2023.

146 Virginia Shroder, 'Orkney and the West African connection', *The Orkney News* (29 June 2020), available at https://theorkneynews.scot/2020/06/29/orkney-and-the-west-african-connection/, accessed on 29 March 2023.

147 adrienne maree brown, 'Murmurations: accountable to our ancestors', *Yes! Magazine* (27 October 2022), available at https://www.yesmagazine.org/opinion/2022/10/27/murmurations-accountability-ancestors, accessed on 29 March 2023.

148 Resmaa Menakem, 'What somatic abolitionism is', available at https://www.resmaa.com/movement, accessed on 29 March 2023.

149 Rhonda Magee, *The Inner Work of Racial Justice: Healing Ourselves and Transforming Our Communities Through Mindfulness*, TarcherPerigee, New York 2019, p.301.

150 King, *Mindful of Race*, p.150.

151 SN 47.19, *Sedaka Sutta*. Adapted from https://suttacentral.net/sn47.19, accessed on 6 April 2023.

152 See https://self-compassion.org/exercise-2-self-compassion-break/, accessed on 29 March 2023.

153 Norman Fischer, 'Nothing to give, no one to receive it', *Lion's Roar* (26 November 2020), available at https://www.lionsroar.com/nothing-to-give-no-one-to-receive-it-norman-fischer-on-joyful-giving/, accessed on 29 March 2023.

154 Rachel Naomi Remen, 'Helping, fixing or serving?', *Lion's Roar* (25 October 2021), available at https://www.lionsroar.com/helping-fixing-or-serving/, accessed on 29 March 2023.

155 MN 53, *Sekha Sutta* (also known as *Sekha-patipada*).

156 Parker J. Palmer, 'Living from the inside out', commencement address, Naropa University, May 2015, available at https://youtu.be/MaOFkumhcCU, accessed on 29 March 2023.

157 Lucy Chan, 'How I saved a life with fierce compassion', available at https://www.ted.com/talks/lucy_chan_how_i_saved_a_life_with_fierce_compassion, accessed on 29 March 2023. Quoted with permission from Lucy Chan.

158 Brené Brown, *Rising Strong*, Vermilion, London 2015. See also Brené Brown, 'Boundaries', available at https://youtu.be/-WpdsRPzKco, accessed on 29 March 2023.

159 A phrase repeated many times in discourses on the brahma-viharas, for example in DN 13, *The Three Knowledges*.

160 AN 6.13, *Nissaranaya Sutta*.

CHAPTER 5

161 Ryokan, *Between the Floating Mist: Poetry of Ryokan*, trans. Dennis Maloney, White Pine Press, Buffalo, NY, 2009.

162 Yang, *Awakening Together*, p.xviii.

163 Pamela Ayo Yetunde *et al.*, 'Ubuntu: I am because we are', *Lion's Roar* (3 January 2022), https://www.lionsroar.com/ubuntu-i-am-because-we-are/, accessed on 30 March 2023, quoted with permission from David W. Robinson-Morris.

164 Rob Burbea, *Seeing That Frees: Meditations on Emptiness and Dependent Arising*, Hermes Amara Publications, West Ogwell 2014, pp.420–1.

165 Video of the Roo-bellion can be seen at https://twitter.com/XrRebel/ status/1181979242852212736, accessed on 30 March 2023.

166 For example the Socratic Paradox: 'I know that I know nothing.'

167 River Wolton, '30 July', in *Year*, p.79.

168 Snp 4.8, *Pasura Sutta*, verses 824–5, trans. Gil Fronsdal, in *The Buddha before Buddhism: Wisdom from the Early Teachings*, Shambhala, Boulder, CO, 2016, pp.71–2.

169 Thich Nhat Hanh, *Being Peace*, Rider, London 1992, pp.11–12.

170 Ajahn Sucitto and Nick Scott, *Where Are You Going? A Pilgrimage on Foot to the Buddhist Holy Places, Part 1: Rude Awakenings*, Cittaviveka Monastery free edition, 2010, p.238.

171 'The image of the Buddha', available at https://pluralism.org/the-image-of-the-buddha, accessed on 30 March 2023.

172 Conversation with Tchiyiwe Chihana (22 February 2023).

173 SN 1.23, *Jata Sutta*, quoted in Vis 1.1, Buddhaghosa, *The Path of Purification*.

174 Conversation with Tchiyiwe Chihana (22 February 2023).

175 DN 16, *Maha-parinibbana Sutta: Last Days of the Buddha*, trans. Sister Vajira and Francis Story, available at https://www.accesstoinsight.org/tipitaka/dn/dn.16.1-6.vaji. html, accessed on 30 March 2023.

176 See https://grieftending.org, accessed on 30 March 2023.

177 Quoted in Maria Popova, 'Einstein on widening our circles of compassion', available at https://www.brainpickings.org/2016/11/28/einstein-circles-of-compassion/, accessed on 30 March 2023. Pronouns changed from he/himself/his.

178 Analayo, *Compassion and Emptiness*, p.116.

179 Ibid., p.58.

180 Joseph Goldstein, 'Liberation through non-clinging', Insight Meditation retreat, Gaia House, June 2009, https://dharmaseed.org/talks/9787/, accessed on 30 March 2023.

181 Tom Robbins, *Another Roadside Attraction*, Doubleday, London 1987, p.28.

182 River Wolton, '26 June', in *Year*, p.68.

183 Name changed to protect identity.

184 William Shakespeare, *The Merchant of Venice*, act 4, scene 1.

RESOURCE 2

185 Salzberg, *Lovingkindness*, p.190.

ABOUT THE CONTRIBUTORS

Zohar Lavie lived in Israel until her early twenties, and has been practising meditation in different traditions since 1995. This journey has taken her from the meditation cushion into exploring further ways of expressing truth and love, and in 2004 she co-founded SanghaSeva. She now spends most of her time facilitating retreats that offer service as a spiritual path around the world. Since 2006 she has been teaching on silent retreats and Dharma gatherings in India, Europe, Palestine/Israel, and online.

Nathan Glyde has been practising and studying meditation since 1997, and sharing teachings on retreats since 2007. In 2004 he co-founded SanghaSeva, whose retreats emphasize wisdom and compassion in ecological and humanitarian service.

Jaya Rudgard began meditating in the 1980s and practised for eight years as a nun in the Thai Forest Tradition in England. She is a graduate of the Insight Meditation Society/Spirit Rock Teacher Training, and teaches Insight Meditation and mindfulness in the UK and internationally. She also studies and teaches qi gong.

Kareem Ghandour is of Palestinian and Lebanese heritage. He grew up in Jordan and moved to the UK in 2008. He is a mentor and director at iBme UK (Inward Bound Mindfulness Education) and has spent many years active in mindfulness initiatives for youth, including the Wake Up movement for young adults, and the charity Youth Mindfulness. He completed his mindfulness teacher training in 2018 with Jack Kornfield and Tara Brach. He is passionate about the role of play, creativity, and social justice in the mindfulness world.

Esther Slattery is a black Londoner, mother of two, meditation/mindfulness practitioner, and teacher. She is also a psychotherapist with special interest in trauma, self-esteem, belonging (identity, equality, and inclusion), and dynamics of wellbeing (including health inequalities). She trained to teach at the University of Oxford (MSt in MBCT). She has been teaching in the community (voluntary and private sector) and within the NHS (staff and patients).

Yanai Postelnik is of European and Asian ethnicity and grew up in New Zealand. He first encountered the teachings of the Buddha while travelling in Asia in 1989, and has been teaching Insight Meditation and Buddhist practice internationally for thirty years. He is a member of the Gaia House Teacher Council, and a Core Faculty member of Insight Meditation

Society, Massachusetts. Much inspired by the Thai Forest Tradition, and the transformative power of the natural world, since 2018 he has devoted a significant amount of time to activism and non-violent civil disobedience, calling for an appropriate response by government to the climate, ecological, and social-justice emergency of our time.

INDEX

Introductory Note

References such as '178–9' indicate (not necessarily continuous) discussion of a topic across a range of pages. Wherever possible in the case of topics with many references, these have either been divided into sub-topics or only the most significant discussions of the topic are listed. Because the entire work is about 'caring', the use of this term (and certain others which occur constantly throughout the book) as an entry point has been restricted. Information will be found under the corresponding detailed topics.

absorption, meditative 84–5, 183
abundance 12, 117
abuse 127–8
acceptance 89, 118–19, 133
Acrobat Sutta 125
activism 8, 17, 22, 144
 inner 158–9
 peace 2, 114–15
activists 11, 80, 114–15, 180
 peace 46–7
addiction 84–5, 167
African Voices Platform 154–6
age 6, 33, 94–5, 108, 120–1
ageing 6–7, 104–5, 176
agency 6, 8, 38, 84–5, 152–3
aggression 94, 158–9
agitation 12, 22
Aida refugee camp 8–9
air 52, 72–3, 90–1, 117, 126, 134–5, 138, 170
Al-Samarrai, Alaa' 10
Aldrin, Buzz 54–5
Alrowwad Culture and Arts project 8–9
altruistic joy 92–3, 183
ambivalence 94–5
Amte, Baba 24
Analayo 120, 165
Ananda 17, 131–2, 163–4, 182
ancestors 96–7, 112–15, 123, 143
anger 61, 68, 74, 76, 88, 174
animals 58–61, 94–5, 120–1, 142
 companions 59, 114–15
Anthropocene 5, 8, 178, 182
anukampa 14, 120, 182

anxiety 6, 10, 52, 58, 68, 146–7, 162, 167
 ecological 8–9
appreciative joy 92, 94, 150
appropriate responses 6, 12, 88, 133, 144, 158, 163
Arkwright, Richard 123
Armstrong, Neil 54–5
artists 8, 30, 114–15, 179
arts 8–10, 154–5
 Alrowwad Culture and Arts project 8–9
 arts and culture activities 154–5
aspirations 11, 31, 52–3, 103, 136, 145, 154–5
attention 12–13, 26–7, 48–9, 68, 76–7, 84, 96–7, 102
Atthakavagga 148
Australia 42, 117, 152
autumn 90–1, 141–2
Avalokiteshvara 42, 182
avijja 149, 182
awareness 26–7, 32–3, 63–4, 79, 84–5, 104–5, 134–5, 138–9

backache 131–3
Baghdad 4, 64–5
balance 15, 24, 27, 70, 150–1, 154–8, 160–1, 183
barriers 52–3, 76, 104, 111, 167
'Beautiful resistance' 8–12
beauty 78, 86–7, 90, 110, 143, 148, 163, 165
befriending 51–81, 116, 171
 blocks 60–2
 and dancing with Mara 67–71

and field of intentionality 63–4
 flowers of hope, fuel of despair 65–7
 friendly/unfriendly reminders 73–5
 and gift of gravity 54–6
 guided meditation 62
 and kindness 57–60
 metta and compassion 80–1
 metta and everything 76–7
 moving metta 71–3
 orientation for life 52–3
 phrases and categories 77–80
Being Peace retreats 26–7
beings 58, 76–9, 81, 84, 108, 110–11, 173–4, 177
 human 41, 66–7, 75, 113, 143, 165–6
 living 31, 52, 61, 111, 174–5, 177
beliefs 16–17, 32, 89, 127, 148, 182
belly 29, 74, 104–5
belonging 24, 94–7, 114–15
benevolence 52–3, 62
Bethlehem 8–9
bhavana 18, 182
biases
 identity-based 30, 124
 unconscious 120–1
BIPOC 17, 96–7, 179, 182
birth 46, 112, 138, 160–3, 167, 182
birthrights 18–19, 111
Black Lives Matter 118
black women 68, 127, 154–5

blackbird 85
Blake, William 104–5
blue sky 64–5
boats 12, 31, 128, 150
bodhisattvas 182
bodily sensations 41, 54, 58
body 24–7, 32–4, 44–5, 54–7,
    60–2, 72–3, 96–7, 134–5
    and bypassing 36–7
bones 36–7, 132
'boundless heart' 14, 79, 111,
    174
boundlessness 104–5, 110–12
Brach, Tara 86, 89
brahma-viharas 14–19, 76–7,
    103–5, 110–11, 138–9, 150,
    152–4, 175
breathing 46, 61, 72, 104–5,
    134–5, 166, 170, 176
Brown, Brené 136
Buddha, see *Introductory Note*
Buddhaghosa 57–8, 77, 182–3
Burleigh, Emma 16
burnout 14–15, 38, 80, 90–1,
    100, 142, 156
    edge of 64–5, 118–19
    parental 6–7
bypassing 36–7

Cahun, Claude 113–14
Cambodia 44–5
care 6–7, 22–3, 35–6, 58–61,
    100–4, 120–1, 137–9, 168–9
    and crisis 5–8
    homes 4, 6–7
    self-care 89
    and time 26–7
    who cares 15–16
carers 4, 6–8
caring 107–39; see *also*
    Introductory Note
carols 86–7
cats 56, 58–9, 63, 77, 86–7
challenges 10, 18–19, 90–1,
    100, 129, 145, 160
Chan, Lucy 136
change, moving for 38–40
charities 38, 118
Chenrezig 42, 182
chickens 58–9, 98
Chihana, Tchiyiwe 7, 154–5
children 6–9, 26–7, 99–100,
    104, 111–13, 123, 170, 174
chocolates 84–5
Christian faith 118–19

circles of connection 112–15
cities 4, 26–7, 44–5, 64–7, 129
citta 133, 182
class 30, 33, 61, 120–1, 129
classrooms 52–3
clay 54–5, 132
climate 6, 8, 11–12, 100, 144
    change 5–6, 8–10, 179
    crisis 12
    emergency 64–5, 152
    protestors 146–7
clouds 64–5, 76, 148–9, 152
collective compassion 117, 179
colour, people of 6–7, 40, 96,
    100, 178, 182
combatants 46–7
comfort 58–9, 89, 129
commitments 2, 22, 80, 124,
    152–3
companions 14, 18, 44–5, 52,
    58, 66–7, 132, 138
    animals 59, 114–15
compassion 41–2, 109–12,
    118–21, 125–30, 133–4,
    136–8, 150–5, 168–9
    in action 120
    collective 117, 179
    definition 117–18
    fatigue 6, 100
    fierce 136–7
    intentions and acts of
        120–1
    and its companions 12–15
    kindling for 103, 105
    and metta 80–1, 150
    for oneself 124–6
    roots 119–21
    sustaining 33, 66–7, 128,
        142–3, 145, 175–81
    thought-police 70, 120–1,
        158, 160–1
    watered by joy's tears 84–5
compassionate actions 30,
    80–1, 131
compatior 119
conflict 2, 38–9, 46–8, 58, 74,
    160–1
confusion 88, 124, 149, 158–
    60, 182
connection 108–10
    circles of 112–15
consciousness 6–7, 28, 68,
    164, 166
contemplation 43, 46–7

contemplative practice 11, 18,
    22, 33, 36, 38–9, 42, 66
contentment 60, 79, 84–5,
    90, 102
contradictions 15, 94–5
cookies 87
corridors 22–3, 133
courage 5–6, 10, 22–3, 104, 111,
    114, 134, 136
Covid-19 6–7, 22, 72–3, 108, 117
    lockdowns 24–5, 72–3, 114
    long 22
craving 70, 137, 183
creativity 4, 8–10, 12, 16, 96–7,
    103, 111, 165
crisis
    and care 5–8
    climate 12
critics 66–8, 70–1
    cruel 66–7
    inner 68, 70–1, 157
cruelty 14, 126, 158
    limitless 58–9
cultural and embodied
        identities 36, 41
cultures 6, 8, 33, 61, 96, 101,
    145, 157
    Alrowwad Culture and Arts
        project 8–9
    arts and culture activities
        154–5
cynicism 70, 72, 88

Dalai Lama 90–1, 101, 146–7,
    182
Daly River region 42
death 54–5, 72–3, 104–5, 113,
    117, 163, 176, 182
Death Café movement 163,
    179
delight 3, 84–5, 89–90, 92–5,
    101, 129, 170
delusion 15, 70, 122, 124, 154,
    164–5, 183
denial 6, 10, 70, 74, 90–1, 146,
    152, 162–3
    of difficulty 84–5
    self-denial 137
depression 68, 86, 89, 99–100
Derwent Valley 123
despair 2, 4, 10, 12, 64–5, 70,
    90–1, 162
    and empowerment 114–16
development of compassion
    52–3

Dhammapada 11–12
Dharma 17, 29, 52, 58–9, 96, 120, 124, 143
difficulty 54–5, 75, 77, 118–19, 126, 130, 158–9
    denial of 84–5
disabilities 22, 33, 70–1, 100, 120–1
disconnection 10, 14, 126, 145, 149, 168
disembodiment 32, 36
disguises 70, 94, 126–8
disgust 126
distractions 40, 77, 129, 158
distress 6, 42, 70, 124, 154, 165
dogs 58–9, 160–1
dukkha 15, 158, 182
Dumfries and Galloway 44–5
dysregulation 33

early Buddhism 68, 120
ears 32, 132, 183
earth 12–13, 31–2, 54–6, 90–1, 96, 134–5, 152, 157
    Earth Vigils 10, 179
East Bay Meditation Center (EBMC) 63–4
ecological anxiety 8–9
edge of burnout 64–5, 118–19
embodied identities 36, 41
emergency 8–9, 152
    climate 64–5, 152
emotional exhaustion 100
emotional regulation 34
emotional repression 3
emotional resilience 70–1
emotions 8–9, 64, 78, 113, 157; see also individual emotions
empowerment 84–5, 96–7, 152–3
emptiness 15, 128, 142, 144, 146
enemies 14, 41, 57, 126–8, 170
enjoyment 70–1, 83–105; see also joy
    backdraught 88–90
    coming home to yourself 95–7
    and envy 92–5
    full range 84–5
    and generosity 101–2
    and gratitude 99–101
    guided meditation 92
    joy in the midst 98–9

kindling for compassion 103–5
opening the heart 86–8
tending joy 90–2
envy 84, 92–5, 152–3
equanimity 14–15, 17, 142, 144, 149–56, 158–60, 162–3, 168–9
ethical precepts, five 175–6
Europe 22, 178
exhaustion 6, 26–7, 30
experience
    direct 17, 33, 58
    physical 38–9
eyes 22–5, 32, 41–2, 46, 48–9, 56, 68, 146–7

fabrication, greedy 158–9
failure 68, 94, 149, 158
faith 10, 114–15
    Christian 118–19
families 14, 48, 53, 58, 108, 113–14, 123, 136
Faslane 365 blockade 5
fatigue, compassion 6, 100
fear 6, 10, 26–7, 70, 88–9, 117, 158–9, 163
fearlessness 104, 175
feet 26–7, 36–7, 40, 46–9, 56, 118–19, 132, 134–5
Feldman, Christina 79
fierce compassion 136–7
fires of greed 15, 124
Fischer, Norman 128
five ethical precepts 175–6
fixity 142, 151, 154–5
Flower Watering 92–3
flowers 14, 64–5, 90–1, 169
Floyd, George 118
fluidity 77, 142–5
food 4–5, 28, 31, 79, 95, 110, 120–1, 160–1
force of gravity 54–5, 154–5
Forest Tradition, Thai 144
forgiveness 66, 75, 92
fortune, good 84, 92–5
Fotheringhame Peace, Janet Fea 112
freedom 26–7, 29–30, 84–5, 102, 104, 143, 165, 167
friendliness 14, 52–3, 57, 59–60, 64, 70–1, 74, 110–11
friends 6–7, 40–1, 66–7, 70–1, 76–7, 90–1, 96–7, 114–15
    good 61, 74, 79, 182

friendship 17, 52–3, 61, 74, 92
    spiritual 92–3, 109, 182

gain 70, 94, 122, 149
Gambo, Rahima 30
gardens 46–7, 72, 109, 117, 120, 133
    school 22–3
gender 61, 100, 120–1
generosity 8, 10, 80, 84, 86–7, 99, 101–2, 128–9
Ghandour, Kareem 17, 86, 89–93, 96, 102–4
gifts 92–4, 99, 101–2, 107, 128, 134–5, 175, 177
    of gravity 54–6
gills 134–5
givers 92–3, 99, 101, 128, 167
gladness 86, 88, 90–2, 173
Global North 6, 108
Global South 6, 109
Gloria Hotel 44–5
Glyde, Nathan 22–5, 29, 32, 35
Goldstein, Joseph 166
Goldthorpe, Mark 8
Gomery, Rabbi Mónica 4
good fortune 84, 92–5
good friends 61, 74, 79, 182
good qualities 92–3
goodwill 41, 52–3, 58, 63–4, 75, 110–11, 182
Google 160–1
Gotama Buddha 69, 131–2, 158, 182
    ancestry 154–5
gratitude 56, 84, 99–101, 116, 177
gravity 146
    force of 54–5, 154–5
    gift of 54–6
Great Turning 6–7
greed 15, 26–7, 57, 70, 80, 124, 154, 158–60
    fires of 15, 124
greedy fabrication 158–9
Greeks 154–5
Gregor, Milla 38–9
grief 8–10, 64–5, 74, 96, 113, 133–4, 163–4, 169
Grief Tending in Community 164, 179
groves 14, 46–7
guided meditations 18–19
    befriending 62

guided meditations (*cont.*)
  caring 115
  enjoying 92
  letting be 169
  pausing 37
guilt 48, 61, 70, 94, 99–100,
  114, 120–1, 142
  and shame 28–9

H4A, see Humans for
  Abundance
habits 12, 29, 60, 77, 114,
  120–1, 124, 126
  patterns 28, 36, 61, 84–5,
  118–19, 160, 168
hamsters 58–9
Hanh, Thich Nhat 3, 86, 108,
  150, 178, 183; see *also*
  Thay
Hanson, Rick 94
Hants, Ann 113
happiness 79, 84, 90–2, 94–7,
  99, 102–3, 175, 183
harm 26–7, 63–4, 74, 77, 80,
  84–5, 127, 129
harmlessness 15, 18, 63, 138,
  146
hate 80, 118, 126–7, 136, 170
hatred 15, 68, 70, 79, 111, 124,
  154, 158–9
head 63, 68, 70, 99, 101, 127,
  150, 160–1
healing 30, 80, 86–7, 101, 131,
  178
health care 24, 41, 100
heart 26–7, 29–31, 83–6,
  89–91, 104–5, 124, 132–5,
  154–61
  heartbeat 24–5
  and mind 26–7, 72, 77,
  84–5, 89, 124
  open 79, 86–8, 158–9, 171
  release 138–9, 165
  supple 133–5, 158
heartbreak 88, 108, 133–4,
  152–3, 157–8
Hellenic art 154–5
heritages 8, 96, 145
Hersey, Tricia 30
Himalayas 154–5
homophobia 35, 40
Hope Mindfulness Centre 47
horse, imaginary 26–7
hostility 152–3
houses 32–3, 46–7, 63, 70–1,
  98, 129, 152

human beings 41, 66–7, 75,
  113, 143, 165–6
human hunger 26–7
humanity 9–10, 66, 75, 118, 143
humans 5, 8–9, 58–60, 123,
  162, 182
Humans for Abundance
  (H4A) 12
humility 43, 66, 114, 118–19, 129
humour 22–3, 70–1, 90–1
hunger 26–8, 70, 126, 149
  human 26–7
Hussein, Saddam 4
hypervigilance 36–7, 41, 152–3
hypocrisy 70, 117

identities 43, 61, 69, 109, 111,
  113, 143
  cultural and embodied 36, 41
  racialized 6, 33, 124
identity-based bias 30, 124
illness 6–7, 22, 70, 162, 166–7
images 14, 32–6, 58–60, 114–
  15, 120–1, 133–4, 154–7,
  160–1
  of compassion 84–5
  self 34–6
imaginary horse 26–7
imagination 46, 56, 110–11, 138
impermanence 104–5, 149
impulses 3, 57–60, 63, 69–70,
  80, 128, 131, 154 5
in-breath 24–5, 32, 40, 145
India 15, 22, 24, 117, 150
Indian subcontinent 154–5
injury 54–5
  moral 6
injustice 2–3, 64–5, 94, 100,
  134, 137, 163, 169
  racial 35, 152
inner critic 68, 70–1, 157
insects 58–9, 138
instruments, musical 118–19
intention
  and acts of compassion
  120–1
  of metta 57, 64, 70, 74, 76
  of non-harm 66
  purer 86–7
intentionality 63–4
Intergovernmental Panel on
  Climate Change (IPCC)
  10
International Space Station
  5, 55
interwovenness 144–5

Iraq 4, 64–5
irritation 24–5, 58–9, 61, 76,
  88, 150
Islamic Relief UK 10
Israelis 46–7
  Occupation 8–9, 103
  settlers 46–7
  soldiers/army 46–8

Jackson, Liz 100
Jaffa Gate 44–5
Jataka Tales 51, 182
jealousy 92–4, 133
Jerusalem 44–6
Johnson, Boris 117–18
joy 14, 17, 84–9, 91–7, 99–105,
  128–9, 154–5, 175–8; see
  also enjoyment
  altruistic 92–3, 183
  appreciative 92, 94, 150
  cultivation 88–9, 99, 102
  ingredients 96–7
  in the midst 98–9
  sympathetic 92–3, 175
  tending 90–2
Joyce, James 36

Kailash, Mount 44–5
kangaroos 146–7
Kannon, see Kwanyin
karuna 14, 120, 182
Karuna News 117, 179–80
Kimmerer, Robin Wall 12–13
kindness 12, 14, 36–7, 52–3,
  57–60, 62, 74, 79–81
King, Angela 118
King, Martin Luther, Jr 110
King, Ruth 79, 124
kitchen 22–3, 72–3
Kornfield, Jack 3, 79, 86, 90–1
Kwanyin 42, 130, 154–5, 182

Laing, Olivia 8
lake 36–7, 79
land 41, 43, 46–8, 109
languages 12, 17, 41, 43–5, 132,
  142, 173, 183
Latin 114, 118–19
laughter 90, 98, 134, 146–7
Lavie, Zohar 22–4, 26–8,
  35, 48
leaping 147–8
legs 36–7, 40, 52, 168
letting be 141–71
  balancing 155–7
  and conflict 160–1